The quest for

Opus Magnum...

Saleem Little

MITANNI
Publishing

The quest for

Opus Magnum...

Saleem Little

MITANNI
Publishing

Saleem Little

Mitanni Publishing
A subsidiary of Mitanni Enterprises LLC
PO Box 13099, Harrisburg, PA 17110, USA

Copyright ©2012 by Saleem Little
ISBN 978-0-9846301-8-9
Cover Design by Saleem Little

The quest for opus magnum

Also by Saleem Little

Get In, Get Out
Love and the Game
Crying For Tears: The Sahsa Pierce Story
Sincerely Yours
Sincerely Yours II: Life, Love & Lyrics
Sincerely Yours III: Gone 'til November
G.O.D.
Special
Black Girl, White World
The Hand That Feeds You
American Made (coming soon)
Dying to Live (coming soon)
Crying For Tears II: The Amina Adu Story
(coming soon)

Table of Contents:

1. Preface...11
2. Evil.....12
3. G.O.D. ...14
4. Tears...23
5. Poems by Alex Domingos...26
   - Lisp
   - Pixie Cut
   - A Patchwork operation
   - Wake & Bake
   - Untitled
6. Fajr...34
7. Cocaine...36
8. To whom it may concern...49
9. Concrete Rose (synopsis)...53
10. Concrete Rose...55

11. Invisible Chains...61
12. The Line...77
13. American Made (Preview)... 87
14. The Moment...90
15. The Motherland...94
16. War is Necessary...96
17. Capitalism (Thoughts)... 100
18. Deeds ..103
19. Bread and Water.....108
20. Pride 109
21. Paradise...110
22. The Bargain...114
23. Think...115
24. Alone...117
25. My Philosophy...118
26. Success...119
27. Special...120
28. Cocoons...201

29. My American Dream...202
30. Mercados...205
31. Careful...207
32. O...210
33. The Great Mistake...212
34. Enemies...213
35. Life After Death...215
36. Legacy...216
37. Acknowledgements.....pg. 217
38. Previews

The quest for opus magnum

"I wanted a perfect ending. Now I've learned, the hard way, that some poems don't rhyme, and some stories don't have a clear beginning, middle, and end. Life is about not knowing, having to change, taking the moment and making the best of it, without knowing what's going to happen next…Delicious Ambiguity."

— Gilda Radner

Saleem Little

Preface

Simply seeking serendipity...this thing has been growing inside of me since I read my first book...this quest consumes a greater portion of my day-dreaming minutes and I am reminded of this trek with each story, each poem, each essay... It is the quest to compose the Opus Magnum...the classic piece of literature...this anthology comprises my humble attempts to compose such a piece...

Saleem Little

Evil

Evil exist in so many forms that its
perception is often a very difficult task.
Religion, philosophy and science ascribe evil to
many entities often to the point of parody.
Although evil may exist in higher levels of
concentration within one single entity, its
ambiance is all-encompassing and ubiquitous.
It can be as overt as unwarranted murder and
as covert as egoism, or, perpetual innate wants
to satisfy the ego; as overt as child molestation
and as covert as materialism...The overt is
easy to notice and curb; the covert not so
much so...

The quest for opus magnum

"If only it were all so simple! If only there were evil people somewhere insidiously committing evil deeds, and it were necessary only to separate them from the rest of us and destroy them. But the line dividing good and evil cuts through the heart of every human being. And who is willing to destroy a piece of his own heart?"

— Aleksandr J. Solzhenitsyn

God

(Preview)

Hamid decided to stay in Afghanistan so he could be with his family for a while. It was something he hadn't been able to do for a very long time. His mother was fifty-two years old now, and though she still retained much of her youthful looks and vigor, Hamid wasn't sure just how long he had left with her. She was becoming very ill. Her cancer was getting the best of her.

The trip had also given Hamid a chance to get back into his Islamic roots. He had truly strayed. He had sought out the consultation of a local Imam and the dialogues he had been having with this sheik was restoring his faith. His biggest question was the concept of God, after traveling the world and being exposed to so many different views.

"Some people say God is an abbreviation for Gomer-Oz-Dabar, a Hebrew term meaning wisdom, strength and beauty." Hamid expressed to the sheik.

"Others say it is no more than an acronym for Gold, Oil and Drugs which is what most people, most notably, Masons and members of the Illuminati apparatus worship."

The sheik pondered these two concepts. He hadn't come in contact with this train of thought but it made much sense to him.

"Well, what I can say is that there is one God, one Universal, transcendent, omnipotent

God. In Islam his name is Allah, which closely resembles the Hebrew Elah in both spelling and pronunciation. Most philosophers and all theologians have a concept of God but it is their polytheistic views of God, or their anthropomorphism of him that lead them astray. They misinterpret the image of the sustainer and creator of life. These people that you say worship God in the form of gold, oil and drugs will make sacrifices for these things which include but are not limited to the murdering of men and women both innocent and guilty."

Hamid thought about the war he was in with Wally. It started over money.

"People will commit haram or forbidden acts like selling drugs, riba, or usury, or businesses that deal in interest. These interests create debt that further impoverishes the already poor."

Hamid thought about Nasser and his opium business. He thought about the drugs Ali supplied. These drugs were destroying the people who consumed them as well as the people that distributed them.

"Then, where you have these religions or ways of life that promote shirk, or attributing partners to Allah, or where people are free to worship prophets, money, their desires; you see people doing just that. They worship idols, these golden calves, and are lead astray from worshipping the one true God. The force that creates the atom, drives the wind, produces the rain, impregnates intelligence in the bee to produce honey that cures sickness in man and is palatable to the taste."

17

"In Hinduism, Brahman is the all-pervasive, eternal, absolute reality in which all things have a beginning and end. However, he is a personified entity that shares divinity with Vishnu and Shiva. So he is no longer one force but three abstract forces that work against and with one another.

"In Christianity, Jesus the Christ – peace be upon him – is the incarnation of God. How this is seen as possible is beyond my understanding considering he prays to God to save him from the pains of the cross and the burden he must bear, the Devil tries to trick him as if he doesn't recognize the creator that barred him from heaven, he sleeps, and eats and bleeds, and somewhere forgets that he is God because he continuously prays to himself. He also says the works he does he cannot do without the father. But if he and the father are one there is no need for distinction or demarcation. So people have begun to pray to him and worship him which takes away from the praise of the one God. In making a man worthy of praise it has led to the praise of Saints, Popes, Mary – peace be upon her - and so many people whose duty it is to serve God, not to be God.

"In the Yoruba religion of West Africa, which is followed by over ten million people there is one supreme God, Oladumare, there seems to be the worshipping of spirits and idols. In Buddhism it seems God does not exist. There seems to be an atheist spirit as there is no God that bestows blessings and administers punishments. There is only the action of man, Karma, and there is no eternal afterlife, only reincarnation where one transforms in life form. Jainism seems to be the same where there is no God, only liberated souls who achieve the status of immortality and omniscience. As we see with the story of the Pharaoh in surah 79, Pharaoh claims that he is God."

"In college there were many people who simply ruled out the possibility of their being a God using the theory of evolution as their evidence against any claims that there was one." Hamid interjected.

The sheik smiled.

"One of Allah's attributes is actually Al-Bari or, The Evolver. Islam does not rule out evolution. Allah Azza wa Jal makes it very plain that there are stages to creation. He is Al-khaliq – the creator, as well as the evolver. The fact that life has evolved from water was revealed to the prophet over fourteen hundred years ago. And Allah has created every animal from water; of them are some creeping on their bellies; some walk on two legs; and some on four. Allah Creates what He wills: for sure Allah has Power over all things. Surah twenty-four, verse forty-five.

"In Surah forty-one, verse eleven Allah speaks of the Big Bang. Stating that the heavens and earth were like smoke and he ordered them to come together willingly or unwillingly. He then shapes them proportionately.

"As far as evolution and Darwin, other men propagated the "Death of God" philosophy; men like Philipp Mainlander and Fred Nietzsche. Many scientist claim that God is a figment of man's imagination and that all of life is matter in motion, ambiguously answering what puts that matter in motion.

Hamid was learning a lot from his consultations with the sheik. Most importantly, he was regaining his inner peace and sense of direction with every solitary and congregational prayer he made.

Tears

She said *"I wanna cry"*...I said, *"that's fine, all I would do is kiss the tears, to taste your pain...to know it...to become one with it...to transform its poisonous effect that destroys to a medicinal one that heals...to isolate it...then...completely erase it. If they are tears of sorrow I'll seek out their source and block it forever. If they are tears of joy, I'll turn the faucet on full blast and break the knob..."*

So why does she cry? Is it because his eyes don't judge, they understand? Is it because she's spent so many nights praying for true love and he embodies a prayer

23

answered and a dream fulfilled? Is it because she could sense the moment was temporary and she wanted it to last forever? Did she curse time and space? Were they tears of joy? Were they tears of sorrow? Were they a salty mixture of both? Was/is she happy or was/is she sad? Is my presence bittersweet? Does it remind of the heights of love's bliss but also the depths of its pain? Is it me or what I represent? Does she love me or is there a void there that any man's attention would fill at this moment?

Why does she cry? Are the tears for *"her"* lifetime or *"our"* moment? Were her tears an Oasis in her emotionally deserted eyes, or merely a mirage created to manipulate my bleeding heart? Was the numbness that blocks emotional release removed by my touch? So many questions aroused by one tear.

24

The quest for opus magnum

She said *"I wanna cry"*…I said, *"that's fine, all I would do is kiss the tears…"*
So she cried…
And I kissed…
I tasted the salt…
It was real…
But was the feeling?

Poems by *Alex Domingos*

Lisp...

pull the string
and surely something
will appear. like
magic, or clockwork
or whatever
such sorcery
sends rays,
like harlots,
splayed suggestively
on sundials
once under cover
of night, watch

The quest for opus magnum

clouds spill
like hastily applied
makeup to weary,
hollow, eyes. life
has never been known
for its light hand or
gentle touch

©Alex Domingos

Saleem Little

Pixie Cut...

*and all the androgynous
girls with the pixie cuts
smoke cigarettes outside
the punk show. winter wind
is insistent in its approaches
and lurks just beyond holes
in knees. the sky crafts
the perfect backdrop
for sinister nights rife
with forgotten names
and numbers*

©Alex Domingos

28

The quest for opus magnum

A Patchwork Operation...

*i found love in
the back of
a taxi when
i saw the future
obscure ripped
upholstery.*

©Alex Domingos

Saleem Little

Wake and Bake...

*Luckily we
have no need
for the sun.
Wiser hands
have crafted
fire in convenient
plastic enclosures,
flavored cotton
candy blue and
high fructose
green. Before
the sun tarnished
the city with
brassy bombast
i left prints
on the tops of*

The quest for opus magnum

clouds. Nearly
fell through silken
floors in a moment
of carelessness but
taunted death
with derisive and haughty
laughter. God made
dirt and dirt aint
worth fucking up
your sneakers
©Alex Domingos

Saleem Little

Untitled...

*the indifferent
measures,
temperature
and time,
spare no pity for
wandering poets.
reluctant muses
hide behind
open palms
and reddening
cheeks*

©Alex Domingos

The quest for opus magnum

$\mathcal{F}ajr$

She awakens
Pleased with Allah's creation
In awe of consciousness
Time for morning meditation
Salaam is her salutation
Submissive contemplations
She performs her ritual cleansing
And I watch her in amazement
In our silence I hear Angel's rejoicing
As she spreads her carpet
Wishes peace to west and east
MorningPrayer has now been offered-
And instead of TV...
She reads, she reads...
Shereads of how he feeds the needs

The quest for opus magnum

She pleads, she pleads
Please provide, I will comply
I am no different than birds in the sky
All things have been fed
All of life has its bread
So I'll take the faith from me
And put the faith in you instead…

Cocaine

Preview

I come from Sabaneta in RepublicaDominicana, a small municipal district in the Puerto Plata province on the north coast of the Dominican Republic. My name is Fuego but my nickname is Perico, it's a long story. In a country where the people depend on Agriculture alone to bring wealth to the economy, I am their hope. Though my dealings are considered illegitimate the people love me because I provide. I make the necessary sacrifices to bring money to this country. Fearlessly my family continues to make the trip to America to earn wages in

American currency that almost doubles in worth when sent back home.

Still, you have those who despise my very creation. To them I'm the bad guy. They claim I am poisoning my country, destroying my own people and to an extent, this is true, though it is not necessarily my plan. I would much rather poison my American Patrons and keep them hooked on what I provide. Not my own, but hey, who said the game would be fair.

I was separated from my mother and father immediately following my birth. This wasn't wise because I was still very fragile and under developed. I had to be placed in an incubator and groomed artificially. I was fed so many different types of drugs and chemicals I was almost complete changed physically. The steroids given to me to restore my strength made me extremely potent. Before that I was just a frail little boy, hardly capable of harming anybody.

My new parents, farmers who worked on a sugar plantation, snuck me in and allowed me to live with them in their two-room shade. It wasn't the best but it was home. A thatched roof and dirt floors, I was reminded of Sabaneta's indigence early in life and vowed to do something about it.

I've been handled by the best and worst alike, wealthy cocaine lords and street corner hustlers, passed around like something useless, wasted, used and abused, stepped on, cut up and burned; I had to get out of this country. I was worth nothing here. So estranged from my parents I could no longer even relate to the state that they were in. I prayed night and day to fall into the hands of a

38

Cocaine Lord who understood my worth and my value in an indolent country that didn't produce workers like me; workers who were immune to the strains of labor and not afraid of a life on the streets. A place like the United States, Home of The Free, where making less than $10,000 a year was considered poor. That comes from being so spoiled, make $10,000 a year in the Dominican Republic and you're richer than two thirds of the country.

There's no secret that the reason we're treated like dirt is because African influence is so strong in my country thanks to neighboring Haiti.Because most Haitians are descendants of slaves from Africa, African custom is still very prevalent in that region. Half of the people here live on farms or work as farmers on large plantations, mainly sugar plantations. And the food they grow buys only the bare necessities. Those who reside in the cities live in crowded old Spanish-style tenement buildings, marked by decay and dilapidation.

Roman Catholicism is wide spread here so most of my people are waiting for something or someone in the sky to come down and change their conditions. Maybe if they weren't so blinded by mythological fables they could see that I was the savior... I am the messiah!The sooner they realize this, the better off they'll be.

The day I've been waiting for arrived soon and I was sold for $900 to a man that swore he would get me into America by any means necessary. I was a slave but I figured once I was in the United States I would buy my freedom or rebel and take it. My plan was to control the world anyway. And it was only a matter of time.

Wrapped tightly and restricted to my narrow confines in the bottom of a boat, I tried to maintain patience. Knowing this would be a long trip. Many die on this trip many are caught, coast guards, naval soldiers, ambushed by other transporters... But coming from where we come from, the risk is well worth it...

Three Days Later...

Darkness...

My eyes processed nothing else...

Sweat drenched my rather pale skin as I tried to twist but me and the others being transported were just crammed too tight. The heat was intense and I prayed this trip would be soon. Oh, the perils of being smuggled into a country. And I prayed even harder that the U.S. coast guards didn't discover me, they keep my people tightly sealed as evidence and then incarcerate us for life or do with us how they see fit. They treat me as some form of illegal substance, labeling me an illegal alien.Although I merely want the American Dream they propose, they label me an immigrant. To them I'm a pestilence, no matter how cheap my labor is…

Right now my only concern is that I make it across the Atlantic and into Miami safely. Many have died on this same journey. But if I can survive, I'll be, in my eyes, free, and able to live the American Dream and also be able to send money back to my people in Nogales, that is the country in Mexico in which

The quest for opus magnum

I was born into extreme poverty. I was separated from my family at birth and have lived most of my young life alone, worth no more than 2-300 dollars. That's it. My friends call me Perico, and the name has stuck considering I knew no name before that.

This is not the first time I've made this risky trip to America I've done it numerous times before. Most of my relatives have as well. It is a trip of desperation. Being poor the risk seems well worth it. Right now the boat is shaking and trembling but me and the four-hundred other Dominicans crammed in the bottom of this boat like Sardines can barely move.

And then...
Light...

Saleem Little

A pair of light tan hands pulled me out of the boat and stared at me as if I was some prized possession.

"Muy Bien" The man says in the language I'm familiar with. As my people embrace me I'm just happy it's not the American Authorities.

The man say I'm a little gringo, or whit boy, but he knows my roots are literally deep in the soil of DR. He kissed me on the cheek, and after the salt from my sweat numbs his tongue, he replies I'm not basura or trash and tells the guy that got us into America he'll put me to work immediately... It was the start of a crazy ride.

My new boss took me home and showed me to my room. I had been in a lot of strange spots before but hey, each man has his own individual tastes. Instead of, under a bed or in a wall, he put me in a giant bowl in the living room under a few potpourri leaves. Go figure.

I wouldn't be here long however. The next day a twenty-one year old Spanish kid from Washington Heights came to take me on a trip to the Big Apple. I was going to see my cousins in New York City. The Drive took about two days, but besides refueling and grabbing food, it was a nonstop trip. The kid had brought his girlfriend and she actually did most of the driving.

Once we arrived in New York my joy was quickly cut short as I was notified that all of my cousins had been discovered hiding in the Harlem basement of a notorious dealer. Unfortunately, I don't have the luxury of entertaining my emotions for very long periods

45

of time. This game is cutthroat and very high risk. I would have to mourn quickly and move on as I was already being placed in the car of a thirty-six year African American man from Brooklyn.

For what it's worth, Hakeem was a pretty cool guy. I don't think his intentions were ever to hurt anybody. He always told me how guilty he felt when he sent me out on hits to collect his money but that he had a family to feed. He had tried to go the straight route but after two felonies, society just wouldn't let him get ahead. What could he do?

I lived for a while and Luckily Hakeem didn't want me to do all the work. He wanted me to relax, make myself at home. He promised to feed me and take good care of me. He wanted me to reproduce. Only if he knew, let's just say…I don't shoot blanks.

When it was all said and done I had thirty-six children. THIRTY-SIX!

Unfortunately, all of their lives would turn out to be living Hells. I get letters from all my children and the stories they tell me are horrific.

1. My oldest daughter Maria was run over by a car tire and killed when her employer was being robbed. Both he and his robber ended up dying that night.

2. Jorge's guilt led him to suicide after killing a pregnant woman and her child.

3. Juan was imprisoned but mysteriously his case disappeared and he ended up living with a local cop in Philly for a few months before

being set free in the Bad Lands section of North Philly.

And that's only the stories of three of them...

To Whom It May Concern...

RE: A message from the youth.

First and foremost, stop blaming us for what we've become. Humans learn through imitation…must we really elaborate? Don't blame us for our values…blame Viacom, blame Google. Blame the creators of Grand Theft Auto and yourselves for allowing us to play it. Blame yourselves for watching those pointless, immoral reality shows knowing we were in the room. Stop cursing in your conversations then cursing rappers for cursing. Your hypocrisy is why we don't take most of you serious enough to heed your advice.

Saleem Little

Maybe when we see you walking what you talk we'll follow your lead.

Stop acting as if you weren't young before, as if you didn't listen to songs you shouldn't have been, as if you didn't sneak into house parties you weren't supposed to. Okay you've matured, now you know the error of your ways, hindsight is 20/20…whatever. If we live long enough maybe we'll get there, but don't forget your youth. Tap into it and you'll be able to relate and deal with us better. Be leaders, fight the evil forces that are influencing our young venal minds…we're not wise enough yet to do it. We don't see the long term effect of our actions…show us, show us, show us…LEAD US! Don't talk to us because basically, we don't wanna hear it. We need to see who you want us to be.

The quest for opus magnum

How can you expect us to be nice, peaceful, and positive when you're combative, argumentative and crude? Have you heard how you all interact with each other? You're always gossiping, slandering, backbiting, complaining, fighting, and screaming. None of you seem to like each other. You kill each other about land and money and religion and race and pride and ego and emotion. And we're younger but we're all humans. We all fall victim to the whims of our lower selves. Stop crying about violence when you promote and endorse it. You get on these social sites and sow the seeds of division. You put people against each other. You have these silly competitions for likes…you're still having high school like popularity contests. Most of you follow whatever the Media says to. You

51

entertain musicians that in your heart of hearts you know don't tap into your soul with their shallow materialism and egotistical pomp. You accept shows that lower your standards and view of humanity. You eat foods that destroy you then feed them to us without an ounce of regret. True, we are the future and will one day lead but you have to lead us there first. We know that if you know better you do better but to know better you have to be shown better...

Sincerely,

The Youth

Concrete Rose

(Synopsis)

The Idea for this particular song was inspired by the works of Tupac Shakur. I've always been a firm believer that although you cannot control where you start you do determine where you end up. Humble beginnings often lead to successful endings. In my environment you pick up habits, customs, slangs, etc. that could be detrimental to your existence. After a while you wake up and you realize that there has to be a better way; a better life out there. Some of us choose to stay the same and some of us strive for change. A rose is a rose, no matter where it grows…even if it's in a concrete garden. If this rose has the strength to survive it can blossom into a flower just as beautiful as one nurtured by the caring hands of a gardener in the finest of soil. Oftentimes, the rose that grows wild is more revered because of the obstacles it must overcome to survive. When placed in an environment conducive to proper growth and development, to flourish is expected and to fail is not ordinary. Contrarily, when failure is expected to flourish is sometimes a miraculous feat.

The quest for opus magnum

Concrete Rose

"Did you hear about the rose that grew
From a crack in the concrete?
Proving nature's law is wrong it
Learned to walk without having feet.
Funny it seems, but by keeping it's dreams,
It learned to breathe fresh air.
Long live the rose that grew from concrete
When no one else ever cared."

Rest in Peace Tupac Shakur...

'What is art, it's my escape/ from my heart,
comes what I say/ tryna ball in Bora Bora, gotta
crawl to walk away/ and my projects' made of

*stone/ nevertheless a seed was sown/ so if you
stop at that crack in the road/ to see what
arose/ you see a rose/ in a concrete grove/
where the obsolete grow/ and the obscene
goes on, I mean, I shouldn't have known/ half
of the things I knew at 9/ yea, a little ahead of
my time/ but, that glamorization of crime/
influenced my young and impressionable mind/
so it was like get up, get out, grind/ then it was,
gotta, get a, nine/ I mean, gotta, get in, line/
guys that was trying to get at mine/ next thing
you know, I'm stuck in a game/ that over the
years corrupted my brain/ first it started witlovin
the change/ I bought me a Range now I'm lovin
the fame/ lovin the women that's lovin my
name/ I bought me a Benz right after the
range/ I did it for Benny in back of his cage/
praying for sunshine after the rain/ telling me,
'Ball and ball hard, for all of them laps around*

the yard'/ again he said 'Ball, Ball, Ball, cause slowly but surely they killin us all...'

'...A chapter has come to a close/ and - a seed has just turned to a rose/ and - those petals resemble the wings on top of a butterfly after it grows/ lights and cameras after the shows/ most of my peers just after the h**s/ I find it hard to take advantage of what I see as lost souls/ I just hope them broads grow/ and pray all my goons can turn into kings/ tho' it's a very unlikely thing/ I'm optimistic and I like to dream/ so may the flow forever increase/ may the dough just never decrease/ and all of my bros and innocent souls on death row I pray you're released/ all of my foes I pray you decease - die/ you can't relate to my peace - fine/ I bet you relate to my piece - nine/ don't care if

Saleem Little

*you're resting in peace - bye/ my life I've been
looking for clo-sure/ the chaotic mind of
compo-sers/ who struggle to keep their compo-
sure/ with women who screw you for Rov-ers/
or girls who give up their hymen/ I'm talking
virginity just for a diamond/ if you're not a
rapper than why are you rhyming/ oh, you a
trapper and that's how you grinding/ you one of
the reasons music is dying/ see, we search for
pots of gold/ but we didn't know when we got
the gold/ that too much gold can rot the soul/ if
the mind is not in control/ and the moral ground
is weak/ then the street beneath your sneaks'/
will open and Hell will tug at your feet/ your
circle of friends will turn into snakes/ and you'll
see that money is all that they lust/ oh what a
sad and lonely fate/ you'll find that your money
is all you can trust/ when the soul has been
sold/ then the heart becomes cold/ but like*

The quest for opus magnum

Coelho, The Alchemist that made your soul
can turn it to gold/ so watch out for Medusa
boy her stare can turn you to stone/ watch out
for microchips presented by evil men who will
turn you to clones/ watch out for Israel's reign/
and Syria's pain/ watch out for forked political
tongues/ and don't become too greedy for
fame " fame " fame/ the high could ruin your
brain/ first they 'ahhin' and 'oohin' ya name/
then they wine and boo you the same/ so find
your lane/ grind for change/ buy you a boat and
sell up the river/ like the LP I delivered/ I'll be
gone 'til November…'

Saleem Little

"Sell your cleverness and buy bewilderment."

 –Rumi

Invisible Chains...

(A short story)

Katrina stands on a corner desperately trying to hail a cab. She clutches tight at her six year old son so he can't run off into the street. They're both soaked in rain and the storm is showing no signs of slowing down. In fact, like every storm Katrina encountered in her life, it only got worse.

The force of the wind blows her umbrella upwards and breaks the thin metal poles that hold it together. Her son watches as she throws it in a fit of anger. Stevie's young mind is having a hard time understanding the complexities of human emotion buthe can feel their force like the winds blowing his body back and forth. Though his prepubescent mind has a lot of developing to do, he senses that the umbrella is a small problem that merely agitates her frustrations with the larger ones in her life.

A cab stops and they both run in haste to settle into the dry warmth of the taxi. Katrina tries hard not to make eye contact with the cab driver as she gives him directions to their destination with her head down. He makes a curious face at her peculiar behavior, then dismisses it as none of his business and drives them safely to their destination.
In fifteen minutes they arrive.

"Thank you" Katrina says while handing the cab driver his fare, her head still hanging low.

"Yeah, thank you" Her son says happily.

"No problem buddy. You take care of ya mother."

The man's concern caught Katrina off guard. She lifted her head and the driver now saw what Katrina had been trying to hide behind the big sun glasses and the silk Fendi scarf.

"You sure you don't want me to take you to the hospital Ms.?"

"No thank you"

"I won't charge you."

"I'm fine, really. I'll be okay, Thank you though "She says while pulling her son out of the car quickly. Katrina hated when people got in her business, no matter how nice they were trying to be. The cab driver watches as she walks to the house and not until she and her son are safe inside does he pull off.

63

Saleem Little

It didn't surprise me when Katrina and Stevie showed up at my door that rainy afternoon in March. This wasn't the first time and I was sure it wouldn't be the last time she'd come to me for protection and consolation.

Stevie already knew the routine. My house was becoming a second home to him. He put his jacket on the coat rack and ran into my bedroom to watch TV while Katrina and I talked. I removed her jacket and hung it on the rack then sat down beside her on the couch.

"Why do you keep putting' yourself through this?" I asked. Nothing escaped her soar, slightly swollen lips but a slow rhythmic breathing sequence that cracked periodically indicating to me that she was ready to cry at any moment. She did. A tsunami of emotion and her eyes began to overflow. I carefully removed the scarf she had on to cover the dark bruise on the right side of her face. She looked away ashamed and I just shook my head. I hate to judge but some people make it hard not to.

After removing her oversized glasses, she hung her head. My hand supported her chin which rose slowly. Her right eye was swollen shut. A line of wet mascara dripped down her cheeks. I wiped it with my thumb, merely smearing the salty tear and make-up mixture across her delicate cheekbone. A puddle of tears accumulated in my palm while I held her chin.

"Marcus… help me" She whispered. What was I supposed to do I thought, she didn't even want to help herself.

"How?" I asked.

"Just hold me." Her words and the sorrowfully pleading tone in which she voiced them reached deep into my chest and pierced my heart. I sincerely hurt for this woman and she was probably the only woman that can make me wear my heart on my sleeve.

Katrina's been the apple of my eye since elementary school. At some point we became too close as friends to cross the line. Not to say we've never thought about or discussed it. Once she had her child we knew we would have to cut ties. We did so for months until that relationship feel through. Again Katrina had come to me but our timing was just never right. This time I was the one in the relationship. Somehow we always managed to stay in touch and I was always available to her if I was single and until I was married and settled down.

The quest for opus magnum

"Why do you keep goin' back to this guy?" I asked examining the bruises up and down her arms, and the smearing make up she used in an attempt to cover the scars on her body.

"I'm afraid to leave." She said into my shirt.

"I have a baby with him and not only that, he's usually good to me and Stevie. It's just that alcohol, when he gets drunk he talks with his fist, maybe it's my fault sometimes... I know you probably think I'm stupid."

"Not stupid, just blind. You have to leave before things get out of hand. And what about Stevie, you want him to grow up around that? Thinkin it's okay to hit women? I'm not always gonna be here Katrina so you need to..."

She put her hand over my mouth and looked up at me with those big beautiful brown eyes and once again whispered

"Just help me."

I walked Katrina up to my room where Stevie was asleep. After looking at him then back at Katrina I couldn't help but think we would've made a good family if she wasn't so blinded by what she thought was love. I took Stevie into the next room and tucked him in tight.

Back in my room, Katrina's vanity had been bruised so badly that she just wanted me to make her feel beautiful again. As I kissed her on her neck I wanted nothing more than to be inside of her, but, as my kisses got lower and I slid my tongue across the top of her breast I opened my eyes to see that my tongue had been caressing a tattoo of a rose intertwined with the name of her abusive husband.

I'm glad I opened my two physical eyes because with that image my third eye was opened as well. Katrina was too vulnerable. I wouldn't have felt right taking advantage of her vulnerability, and sleeping with her with her mind in this condition. And although this was the day I had been waiting for since the 5th grade, I had to control myself. Discipline is what separates a man from a boy. So I just held her that night. Besides, my comfort was all she really wanted, I didn't want her to feel like she was obligated to sleep with me in return for my continuous support.

The next morning Katrina was gone. In her place there was a note she had written on a piece of toilet paper. She had obviously rushed through it, afraid that I would wake up which would force her to explain to me why she was going back, face to face. The note read:

Marcus,

    Thank you for always being there for me when I need you most. And thanks for not taking advantage of me. You're the best.

                Love always,
                Katrina

    Not even a week later and Katrina was calling me and once again she was crying. She had been beaten again and now finally realized that she had to get out of that environment.

"He's gonna kill me Marcus. I don't know what to do; it just feels like the walls are closing in on me."

Once again I just asked,

"Why did you even go back?" This whole thing was getting redundant.

"He said he wanted to work it out for the sake of Stevie. He said he would get counseling. I just thought..."

She began speaking in broken sentences.

"I want to be gone before he comes back again... I... I want to get out of here... Marcus, I need to get out of here..."   The last part of her statement had drifted off and right before I could tell her I was on my way, I heard his voice.

"Who you talkin to Trina?" He asked angrily

"Nobody"

"Who da hell is this?" He asked me after snatching the phone fromKatrina. I heard Stevie begin to cry.

"It's Marcus Man..."

I really didn't know what to say.

"What's wrong with you hittin on her like that?" I barked. I was already angry that Katrina had involved me in her quarrel.

"Why don't you mind ya damn business, what you worried about what I do with my woman for anyway?" He shot back. I tried to answer but before I could he ended the call. Maybe it was a twist of sadistic fate but he never hung up the phone. So, I listened intently

72

as the moment I dreaded since Katrina first met Stevie's began to transpire.

"Who da hell is Marcus Katrina?" he barked. I could tell he had moved closer because when Katrina responded,

"He's just an old friend of mine." Her voice shook as if the loud thumping of her heart was causing her voice box to tremble. They went into a serious of screams and taunts until eventually Katrina yelled out to Stevie,

"Go pack your stuff up baby we're leaving."
All of a sudden this big bad man sounded like a hurt, vulnerable little boy. He began to plead…

"No baby, you can't leave me; I'm nothin' without you; I love you; I need you; I promise I won't hurt you again…"

For a minute I thought Katrina was really going to fall for his bullshit again until I heard,

"No Jimmy, not this time. You haven't changed yet and I've finally realized that you never will! And because you don't care if our son sees you like this, I have to be the one that does! I'm leaving!"

I smiled a selfish smile. I was happy that she had finally come to her senses and stood up for herself. But my smile was quickly replaced by a look of terror as I heard Katrina and Stevie begin to scream. Stevie's screams were the loudest as he yelled,

"No, Don't kill my mommy, please...Don't shoot her."

I felt helpless. Katrina's house was twenty minutes away. I could've made it in fifteen if I floored it, but that still may have been too late. Still, it was worth a try. But when I got my coat I heard a gunshot. I looked down at my phone hoping that sound wasn't what I thought it was, but when I put the receiver to my ear I heard Stevie pleading for his dead mother to get up.

"Wake up mommy." He cried

"Wake up…"

As I sunk down in my chair full of despair and guilt, I heard another shot and Stevie's pleading and crying stopped instantaneously. Tears began to flow from my own eyes.

"Not the baby too" I thought. Stevie was innocent. He had nothing to do with… He was only… He… My mind was too scattered to even complete the questions it wanted to ask. I heard the pathetic cries of a grown man at the end of his rope.

75

Saleem Little

"If I can't have you, nobody can."
After that, a third shot and a deathly
silence was all I heard...

The quest for opus magnum

The Line

Sakina had realized that the world wasn't white or black. It was a prism of radiant colors. It was a place where all people could live in unison if they let go of their prejudices and preconceptions. If closed minds would only open and accept that their preconceived notions may just be inaccurate, erroneous, and wrong. All she had seen was one-sided blackness and one-sided whiteness. Not all blacks were lazy, marijuana smoking, welfare recipients. And not all whites were privileged, racist, bigots. The human plight of pain was ubiquitous and not at all exclusive to any one race of people. It, pain, likes its counterpart, joy, is experienced by all people and if people would realize this they could laugh together as well as cry. They would relate to the joy of others and empathize with their pain.

After her internal awakening, Sakina had devoted her life in an inconspicuous manner to prove that fear was bad because it led to prejudices and misconceptions. She wanted to prove, on the other hand, that courage was a good thing because it led to discovery and stemmed from selflessness. She wanted to prove to herself and others that ignorance was evil and stemmed from fear and that knowledge was good because the more you knew of nature's complexities, the more you realized how small and insignificant a role you played in the big scheme of things. This realization would lead to humility. Humility

The quest for opus magnum

would lead to empathy and empathy would
lead to harmony; harmony amongst the races
and amongst all of existence.

Saleem Little

"Your task is not to seek for love, but merely to seek and find all the barriers within yourself that you have built against it."

–Uknown

American Made

(A short Story)

Prince George County, Maryland1973

The night air was brisk; its frigid chill blowing like invisible ice; howling like a wolf enchanted by the glow of a pale full moon. Nothing was extraordinary about the night however; the moon was far from full. In fact, the slim crescent hung in the sky like a discarded, clipped nail. Nine hooded men, completely oblivious to the charms of nature at the moment, spoke in whispered tones; the

81

Saleem Little

breath escaping their cool lips as thick as
storm clouds rather than the normal fog that
rises from a warm breath espoused to cool air.
Though the biting, arctic-like wind on this cool
December night was frigid enough to crystallize
the blood, each man was insulated by a
gushing surge of adrenalin and excitement. All
nine men were revolutionary to the core and
the premise for tonight's plot was something
they had waited their entire tenures as Black
Panthers to manifest.

Staring at the police station that housed
their target, the men gripped tightly at the cold
steel that was pressed firmly against their
palms. As their gloved fingers cradled their
handguns, they thought about the racist cop
that had killed that twelve-year-old girl in the
small town of Woodlawn, two weeks prior.
While this hate fueled their intrepidness, this

plan, and the gravity of its consequences, had heightened their senses. Their hearing was as keen as a bat's; every sound that night was detectable to them. Their eyes cut through the darkness as surgically as those of a cat's. Tacitly, an agreement was made that each man would be given a few seconds more to gain control of any jittering nerves and butterflies, and then they would proceed with the plan. A plan that was simple enough; murder Sergeant Caldwell and anyone that got in the way.

     The men began to move. Stealthily, they stalked towards the entrance of the police station like a group of lioness on the prowl. They glanced around the perimeter of the building; no one was watching. One man took the lead. He walked into the precinct first. He took note of the receptionist, the guards at their cluttered desk, and the inmates in the holding cells, then, Sergeant Caldwell. The man who had entered first raised his. 38, Caldwell's eyes flew wide open and instead of his hands reaching down for his weapon, they shot into the sky in a surrendering gesture. A bullet landed in the center of his forehead sending him crashing to the ground. The shooter had heard nothing but his heartbeat and breath, before the erupting blast of his gun. Now the noise processed it was the shuffling of paranoid feet. Some officers ran for cover while others began to return fire. The man who had killed Sergeant Caldwell glanced back to see his comrades firing at everything moving. Papers flew everywhere, secretaries screamed as an incandescent trajectory of bullets erupted from the smoking, volcanic mouths of the firing pistols like fireworks. Inmate in the holding cells watched in shook.

Sergeant Caldwell's killer noticed the large key ring full of rings and headed towards the body, ducking bullets. He looked up for a second and watched an officer trying to run for a back exit before being stood up by a bullet that cracked through his shoulder blade, then another that lodged itself in his right ventricle. It was obvious that his heart had stopped immediately because he dropped in the same fashion that Caldwell had but bled noticeably less. The man retrieving the keys from Caldwell's belt stood up and opened the door for the inmates in the holding cell.

"Let's go, let's go. Get out of here and hurry up!"

Everyone in the cell stood up and hurried out of the cell, all except one, a middle-aged German man with the tip of an amateur swastika tattoo sticking up out of his shirt collar. The man, who had just shot the brains out of the back of the head of a racist cop, stared at the man for a brief second. The man didn't know what to do, run, or back up into a corner. He didn't know if he was next. The shooting had come to a cease.

"C'mon man, we gotta go. Lock that cracker's ass back up!" One of the panther's comrades called out to him. He smiled and shook his head.

"Must' be ya lucky day ..." The Panther said still fighting back the urge to take Hitler's life.

"Go'on and get cha ass outta here. You just remember me when you get the notion to harass, beat, or kill a black man, woman, or child. You understand me?"

A stone look of seriousness had washed over the his face towards the end of his warning. The white man just nodded his head, carefully though; afraid if the man saw the swastika on his neck he would rethink his decision. After nodding an appreciative nod, the man took off, thankful his bowels and bladder hadn't betrayed him like they had been threatening to do the moment he saw the malevolent looks in the ebony eyes of the nine hooded men enter the precinct.

"Ay white boy!" Caldwell's killer called to the tattooed prisoner just as he made his way to the entrance of the police station. For a second, the guy thought about not even turning around. He did however, and his bladder began to loosen again. He took note of the sinister smirk on the man's face. He raised his head and cast a questioning look.

"Make sure you tell ya friends about me."

The quest for opus magnum

"The artist is a receptacle for emotions that come from all over the place: from the sky, from the earth, from a scrap of paper, from a passing shape, from a spider's web."

– Pablo Picasso

Saleem Little

The moment

*"We were meant to live for so much more,
have we lost ourselves..."*

I was turning the dial on my radio when I stumbled across these lyrics,

*"Fumbling his confidence and,
Wondering why the world has passed him by,
Hoping that he's meant for more than,
Arguments and failed attempts to fly
We were meant to live for so much more,
Have we lost ourselves?"*

90

The lyrics caught my attention so I continued to listen. It was a song by the band "Switchfoot" and the song was called "Meant to Live" I paid close attention to the message...

"Dreaming about Providence and,
Whether mice or men have second tries,
Maybe we've been living with our eyes
half open
Maybe we're bent and broken..."

Our lives seem to be daily searches for temporary highs; another high just to get us through the day. In our pursuit of escapism we lose sight of the big picture, the ultimate goal, henceforth, we lose sight of ourselves.

"Have we lost ourselves?"

Saleem Little

So many people sell themselves short
not realizing that they were meant to live for so
much more. It pains me to see potential
Genetic engineers lying in alleys, begging for
loose change, Grammy singers prostituting,
soliciting their bodies for next-to-nothing,
Mathematicians peddling heroin. Regret
consumes these people on their death-beds as
they realize they failed to maximize their
existence by not exercising their potential and
cultivating their gifts and natural talents.

Live your life to the fullest, they say life
is like a coin, you can spend it however you
want but you can only spend it once. That and,
you only live once but if you do it right, once is
enough. Both suffice to help my point. This is
the only time you'll dwell in your current body,

so manifest its utmost potential. Don't miss your boat and keep in mind:

"We were meant to live for so much more..."

Saleem Little

The Motherland

Never tasted the motherland, never touched the soil, never smelled the air, or the sweat from the toil, never heard the sounds of the Serengeti, or felt the energy of the Asili, saw severed limbs, from colonizers, who exploited her cities, never watched a child walk a mile for fresh water, if not from the comfort of my home, but I felt it in my bleeding heart, and knew that it was wrong...that pathos aroused in me a bitterness indescribable and made me want to console my mother...

The quest for opus magnum

"*I didn't have to think up so much as a comma or a semicolon; it was all given, straight from the celestial recording room. Weary, I would beg for a break, an intermission, time enough, let's say, to go to the toilet or take a breath of fresh air on the balcony. Nothing doing!*"

–Henry Miller

Saleem Little

War is Necessary

"It's a blessing to die for a cause because you could easily die for nothing."

To live is to fight and to fight in a social setting, the moral of the troops must be high and the solidarity and camaraderie must be cement. Without a unified front, defeat is imminent. The same is true for an individual. Heart and mind must be of one accord. Thought, speech, and action must all be one. Physical and mental health must be consummated by equilibrium. All anatomical properties must be united. The axiom: "The power of the wolf is in the pack", ipso facto, summarizes the value of unity. In order to maintain unity, the confederacy, whether that be an army of men or the faculties of the mind and body – must have a common goal that is greater than the sum of individual objectives.

"In classical Chinese political ideology, military strategy was a subordinate branch of social strategy. Accordingly, the first line of natural defense against disruption of order by external or internal forces was believed to lie in the moral strength of a united people."

-The Art of War

Saleem Little

Even if the cause you fight for is self-preservation (health and well-being), you should fight valiantly and with the valor of a man that may die if he fails to win because you just may. Life is war, no matter how many utopic poets, writers, and philosophers may persuade you to believe otherwise. To maintain peace is to fight off chaos, and therefore a battle must take place. To pick roses one must respect thorns. To eat healthy one must deflect the onslaught of poison food consumption and the instinctual lust to indulge in these bitter sweet foods.

In conclusion, I'm a promoter of peace, but I do realize the natural order of things; the laws that govern the universe. Matter and energy is governed by entropy which is a natural propensity to dissipate. So, all energies are prone to chaos and actually more comfortable in this state. So in order to control this chaotic nature of life, we must fight internal warsin order to maintain discipline, sustain peace, and live in a civilized manner.

If peace is the objective, War is necessary…

"Inspiration may be a form of super-consciousness, or perhaps of subconsciousness -- I wouldn't know. But I am sure it is the antithesis of self-consciousness."

– Aaron Copeland

Saleem Little

Capitalism

What is Capitalism? It is capitalizing on the inferiority or piousness of others to maximize capital. It is a profit driven system that leaves very little room for morals or apathy (empathy). It is an egocentric system that completely contradicts harmonious living. It is a system that divides, deprives, deceives and lies. The man successful in this system is not the strongest, smartest, or wisest... No, the most successful in this system are the most deceptive, dishonest, selfish, morally aloof and apathetic. It is run by men whose flattery is condescending, whose smiles beguile and conceal the vile nefarious nature that drives greed. It is this system that has inevitably led to the collapse of many great civilizations. No True Religious person can thrive in this system because in religion your taught to be honest, to share, to treat others as you wish to be treated, to feed the poor and needy, to shelter the orphans, to avoid usury, interest, credit and manipulation. In short, it is a system that was created by selfish, greedy, minds and no truly Creator-fearing person will ever thrive in this system. As far as atheist are concerned... This is why Eugenics seems necessary not evil and why the Earth is being deprived of its beauty and natural resources. To kill to ensure profit is deemed acceptable in this system, i.e. Native Americans, African slaves, child prostitutes, wild life, animals etc. Because these are all viewed as a lower class species, exploiting,

Saleem Little

even murdering them is not wrong it is merely
a necessary step to ensure "Manifest
Destiny"...

So what is Capitalism? More often than
not it is preying on the weak. If that's not wrong
to you you'll excel. If it is wrong seek
contentment because you probably won't be
too rich....

Deeds

Are we satisfied? Will we ever be? Not as long as we succumb to the insatiable nature of the Ego. The Ego is never satisfied; greedy and always thirsty for more. As long as we covet bravado, arrogance, and look down upon humility and submissions. We will never know peace and serenity; Tranquility and Bliss. As long as we chased fads, as long as we love to show off, as long as we allow ourselves to be duped by insidious marketing ads, we will never be satisfied. As long as we post pictures on social sites with excessive make up and worthless, insubstantial materials so we can feel superior to others we will always be inferior. We will go to our graves wanting more. Even skyscrapers can be destroyed by strong winds so why waste so much time building something that mother nature and father time will inevitably destroy? Why not cultivate good deeds? They're the only things that truly last forever.

Bread and Water

Besides a few egotistical wants, life's basic necessity is bread and water and all of existence is actively engaged in the pursuit thereof. I used to wonder why some get fed and others don't. I would ponder this question often andas it normally happens in periods of silence and meditation the answer to my problem found me. God is subtle and so are his messages and signs. In chaos in turbulence they're hard to see but in complete silence and submission the signs are very visible.

Saleem Little

I watched as a squirrel pulled an acorn from the tree and fed himself. The tree leaves shone brightly in the sun light as the tree absorbed its food; sun rays while drawing water from the ground. Birds flew by and stopped to scour the ground for food. In watching this cycle of life I realized something. 1st, all creatures have been provided with food. Now besides vegetation, most creatures must work for their food but their food has been provided for them by their creator nonetheless. 2nd I learned humility. Because of our comprehension level we believe that our human minds are in control so at times we stress ourselves trying to provide what has already been provided for us. Your food has been provided just follow you're given gifts and talents and you'll obtain your food (wealth) easily. Michael Jordan once said he didn't chase endorsements; they chased him. Instead of trying hard to get a deal to ensure his own sneaker, he simply applied his natural talent and perfected it and that's what made him an endorsement magnet. His life was about sports and becoming the best at his particular sport. He didn't go to school or dream of being a business man. Because society has become so money and materialistically driven artist, entertainers, athletes etc. want to give off the impression they have business savvy as well as skill. Too often however the pursuit of money pollutes the pursuit of cultivating one's talent so as endorsements increase talents decrease...

Back to the porch...

Saleem Little

These creatures humbly submit and are fed and well taken care of. What makes us think we are any different?
Maybe if we listen to our own instincts instead of outside sources telling what we must be, we would be at peace like the rest of creation.

The quest for opus magnum

Pride

Tried to swallow my pride
But it was too bitter
So I threw it back up
And I told her I can't forgive her
And if the sayings true
Thentrue, I'll never forget her
Probably put her in a song
Andwash her down with some liquor
Burn, baby burn, I could put her in a swisher
Now my world is up in smoke
And that's what pride will get cha...

Saleem Little

Paradise

Welcome to Paradise
Where mirrors are forbidden
The truth becomes our fiction
And our fiction our addiction
Where reality's suppressed

The quest for opus magnum

And we drink away the pain
Take psychedelic trips
To Neverland and never land
And never plan because well
Y.O.L.O. is the Motto
No religion's the religion
Virgin Mary's now a model
Velvet floors &fuchsiaceilings
Purple clouds and red streams
Of intoxicating spirits
Renegades of Elohim
Let's play pretend…
For what is paradise?
But vein fantasies
Of man's lust for vanities
Rambling enchantingly…
Debauchery's the order…
Drink up, drink up

Saleem Little

A fashionable accessory bring a cup
But,
Sip it slow…
        Too
                Fast
And
Ya
Heart
May
Stop…
…judging, we're in paradise
Uninhibited by vice
We make the right seem wrong
And the wrong seem right
We bathe in the flames
For to bathe in the rain
Is to bathe in our pain
To save face, we don't face
We don't face the east

The quest for opus magnum

Why?
Well,
Although the West is a mess
It's just...
To live without
Rules, takes a lot less stress
So Yes...
We know our heaven is a lie
But heaven's a state of mind
Why wait for heaven in the sky...

The Bargain

The majority of the people on this planet have succumbed to their lower natures, so to entertain them, to please them; you have to sensationalize the ignorance that has become so blissful to them. The question will always be *"Is it worth your soul to entertain the evil natured?*

The quest for opus magnum

Think

A friend told me that I think too much
So I thought again, and thought…
I don't think you think enough
See, I think about the devil,
And I think he's my opponent
So I'm thinking like a rebel.
Yes, I'm thinking every moment,
So as I think of atonement.
My prayer rug I'm on it
Salat becomes nirvana
That divine moments golden
Tarnished by those evil thoughts
Shortly thereafter,
Live for the here and now

Saleem Little

Or, for the hereafter…
A man told me he was God
I said that cannot be
You're a slave to the same banks
That funded Nazis -
I know the Ten Percent
Who profit off the ignorant
God leads to paradise
You lead them to the liquor dens
Material consumption
And the evil world of dividends…

Alone

Woe to the man afraid of himself, afraid to be alone for fear he will never find peace in his own thoughts… People tend to speak when the silence of their thoughts begin to antagonize them. They seek company when their loneliness drives them mad. How sad is the man whose guilty conscious has made him afraid to be alone.

My Philosophy

All the words have been written, there truly is nothing new under the sun. Ahh, The wisdom of Solomon, Peace be upon him. Oh Adam what did you see? Then the Truth, manipulated over the ages through countless stages, by countless sages, from Pharaoh to Fard, from Elijah to Elijah, Einstein, Newton, Sires have expired while the whimsical desires are the drivers of the liars, your facts are mere conjecture...

Success

Have you ever noticed how when people describe success its always flowery adjectives about materialistic consumption? Images of success are cars, giant houses, shoes, clothes, etc. Even if it's a career path. Making it into the career of choice is not enough. If you don't make a certain amount of money through it then you have yet to achieve success. Not many souls achieve ultimate success or live up to their own standards. What may look like success to one man may be the beginning steps to success for another. However, if we track the insatiable souls of humans we find unrest and feelings of....

119

Saleem Little

When I began my writing career my goal was merely to write a book... I succeeded. After writing a book, my goal was to publish it. Again, I succeeded. After publishing, the goal was obviously to sell some books... I succeeded. The problem stems when the "sum" of some books doesn't reflect..Worldwide mainstream success. Now, if I stop at this point, I may become dejected, feeling as if my goal hadn't succeeded. But that is the ungrateful nature of men. I wrote the book "Success", I published the book, "Success", and I sold a few thousand, "Success" why in the world would I then feel unsuccessful? If I allow the sales of other authors be the tape by which I measure myself two things could happen, both to my detriment. I can become, arrogant or insecure. I may feel superior or inferior. There's never contentment in the mind of the man who is competing with the accomplishments of others... Contentment is not to be confused with complacency. Contentment is merely finding peace, happiness, and joy in any situation you're in. Complacency is feeling you've accomplished all you can and need to accomplish, and resting on your laurels.

Special

THE PROLOGUE:
SCENE I

He read me poems while he talked spiritedly about the life in him that had awakened since meeting me. Staring me in my eyes he read the words…

She's in the house
She's at turn after turn
She's behind me
She's in front of me
She's in my bed
She's on path after path

And I'm weak from want of her,
O heart,
There is no reality for me
Other than she, she, she, she…"

"I swear I could sue him for plagiarism Sophia." He had said so playfully.

I became his new existence; I was his breath of life, the only color in his black and white world.

"You're ruling the way I move, and I breathe your air…" Sade had sung to him and her romantic sonnets became the ambitions of his inner romantic. His dream woman would personify the lyrics to his favorite Sade songs…I was the embodiment of those lyrics to him.

We fought once. I said *"You don't really know me."*

"He said "I beg to differ."

I said "Why is that?"

123

He said "To say I don't know you is to say I don't know myself. We're one in the same."

"How do you figure?" I asked.

"How do you figure we're not?" he shot right back.

Not in the mood to play his game I said, "I have a past."

He simply said,

"And so do I. Every rose has its thorns, and he who wants a rose must respect the thorns. One of the most admired flowers can also be one of the most painful...like love..."

Dante was deep. I always wondered if she knew that side of him. O well, I did, and that's all that really mattered. We would have run away together, I know it but she took him away from me before I could tell him that he too had brought me back to life.

THE PROLOGUE

SCENE II:

Death

His chest heaved...and then...it stopped. His last breath, warm but chilled by death and fogged by the mixture, blew slowly onto my face after I shot him. *"Lena"*, he cried..."*I'm sorry*" he pleaded. And then...he was no more. That scent...mortification...it would stain the fibers of my brain and the hairs of my nose and I would smell the death of Dante forever...My eternal punishment for taking the life of the man I loved...forgive me...

PART ONE:

Curiosity

Dante shot a quizzical look at Lena. This had to be a setup. There was no way she was asking him this with no ulterior motive or hidden agenda. She had to be asking merely to gauge his response. Dante knew he had to be very careful with his response.

"Listen Lena, if this is one of your little test to see how much I love you…"

"No, no…" Lena interrupted.

"I promise it's not a test. I really wanted to know. I've been thinking about it for a while now. I was actually hoping you wouldn't get mad at me for suggesting it."

"Mad at you?" Dante thought. He had actually been thrilled by the idea. Like most men, and women for that matter, he had long given thought to what a threesome would be

like and in his twenty-seven years had yet to experience one. To have two women at once was probably at the top of any man's list of fantasies. Considering suggesting it may have been seen as a sign of mental infidelity, he had never built up the courage to ask. Dante had always been very committed to his relationship with Lena but was very much interested in her idea. No matter how interested however, he reminded himself to maintain his composure and conceal any excitement.

"I mean, you know, if that's something *you* want to do, if it would make *you* happy...I guess I would be cool with it."

Lena smiled.

"Stop it Dante, you know you've thought about it before."

"Maybe once or twice..." Dante said smiling. He could see that Lena was onto his game.

"Yea right, I bet more than twice."

"You're probably right, maybe three times." Dante teased.

Lena shook her head and playfully rolled her eyes at him.

"Ok, you're right, so I have thought about it before, quite a few times, what man hasn't?"

"Have you done it before?" Lena asked, her expression turning serious.

"No."

"Don't lie to me Dante. It's not like I'll be mad."

"*It's not like I'll be mad…*Why do women say that knowing that if what they hear is not what they *want* to hear they *will* get mad?"

"Just answer the question."

"I did, I said no. I've thought about it before, yes, but I've never actually gone through with the act before."

"Ok, I believe you." Lena said.

"So this would be a new experience for both of us then?" She asked still seeking a little more confirmation that Dante hadn't done this before.

"Yup...cross my heart, hope to die." Dante smiled and finally, Lena did as well.

There was silence as they both began to imagine what the experience would be like. Dante hoped the other woman would be just as beautiful as Lena and Lena hoped the same.

Dante glanced over at the *King* magazine Lena had been reading and felt the need to internally thank the vixen on the cover: Nicki Minaj. Obviously the idea had been prompted by her reading of Nicki Minaj's article. The thought may had surfaced a long time ago, it's not unusual for women to be attracted to the beauty of other women, but the trending nature of bisexuality was making more women comfortable with admitting their curiosity and more so, acting on it.

Lena broke the silence.

"So it's settled then, we're definitely gonna try this?" She now seemed to be just as excited as Dante was pretending not to be.

"Guess so..."

"Well, I think we need to lay down some rules."

"Laws for a lawless act..." Dante said sarcastically under his breath.

"What did you say?"

"Nothing."

"What did you say Dante?"

"Nothing baby, what are the rules?"

"Whatever...Ok, listen, she has to be clean."

"Well that goes without saying."

"She has to be pretty."

"Ummm...I think that's an unwritten rule luv." Dante said, unable to contain his laughter.

"Give me a break, I didn't plan this weeks ago, I'm coming up with these as I go." Lena said.

"Ok, I gotchu…next rule?"

"This is a one night thing. We do it then we walk away. I don't care how much we like it, it never happens again."

"Fair enough."

"I'm serious Dante. I'm sure you'll like it even more than me but once it's done it's done!"

"Ok Lena."

"I get to pick the girl."

"What? Wait, why do you get to pick the girl?"

"Because I have to be comfortable with the situation. You're a man, you'll be fine with anything and I might not like your taste."

"Wait, what's wrong with my taste? I picked you didn't I?"

"We picked each other."

"Yea, well *we* can pick this girl together too."

"Ok, whatever...hmmm, I'm scared to see what you would have been with if you weren't with me."

"What?" Dante said unable to make out the last part of Lena's mumbled sentence.

"Nothing. Moving on...I'm not going down on her."

Dante smiled.

"I thought that was part of it but, ok, whatever."

"You're not either."

"C'mon Lena. Why are you trying to put so many limitations on this thing? Next you'll say don't kiss her; maybe don't look at her and the lights have to be off. If that's the case we might as well not even go through with it. Look, it's one night of fun. One night where we let go of all the rules, all inhibitions and just have fun. The point is this is for *one* night, so why not go

132

all out that *one* night and enjoy ourselves unencumbered by rules and limitations?"

"Well, I'll...*we'll* just go with the flow and see what happens I guess."

"Now that's more like it."

"Wait. One more thing..."

Dante rolled his eyes.

"You're never to see or speak to this woman ever again after this is over."

"You said that already Lena. Relax. It's just an experiment. When it's over, it's back to me and you against the world. My love is only for you Lena...I promise."

Saleem Little

PART TWO:

The Prey

In the next few days after Lena and Dante's decision to try their sexual escapade they had actually come to realize that neither really had the nerve to approach a total stranger with such a proposition. No matter how *"sexually free"* people appeared to be these days, the thought of offering one's spouse still felt slightly taboo for them.

Fate however would bump into them and relieve them off the often arduous task of designing one's own destiny. They would not meet their *"prey"* in cinematic fashion, nor at some romantic place like a park or lake. Instead, Lena finished her spicy chicken sandwich and asked Dante to excuse her form their two seat booth at Wendy's. It was in this

134

restroom where she would meet the woman who would soon fulfill their fantasies.

Sophia held the door for an elder woman than braced her steps to match the woman's lethargic pace to the counter to order food. After counting at least ten customers she figured she had time to use the restroom quick and probably not lose much time.

Dante glanced up in time to see the nicest backside wrapped in the tightest blue jeans. He couldn't see the face but the figure said it all.

"Damn..." He thought, never once thinking this could be the woman to complete him and Lena's fantasy. No, his thoughts were much more selfish at the moment...

"Oh I'm sorry," Sophia said, accidentally bumping into the woman who was exiting the bathroom as she was entering.

135

"It's ok" Lena said, not really wanting to look the woman in the eye; embarrassed that the brush was her fault.

Sophia noticed the woman's earring had fallen and decided to get it to her before using the restroom, why take a chance on the woman leaving before she was finished?

"Excuse me." Sophia said as Lena and Dante were leaving.

"Yes?" Lena asked.

"You dropped your earring Sophia said smiling.

"I knew it" Dante said to himself..."I knew there was no way that face wasn't going to be beautiful."

"Oh thank you"

"You're welcome, you're very beautiful" Sophia said unable to tame her crush.

"Umm thank you" Lena stuttered sensing attraction in the compliment.

Dante's light bulb went off.

"Excuse me..." He interrupted.

"Please don't be offended, but are you...
into women?"

"Lena was shocked at Dante's
bluntness. Sophia wasn't.

"I think women are very, very beautiful."

She responded without hesitation and
by the second *"very"* Sophia eyes had cut and
locked in on Lena's. Lena was hypnotized.
Dante was aroused before saying,

"Would you mind if we ate with you..."

Rationale is rarely able to curtail
emotional impulses. It seems at times as if the
heart controls the mind not the other way
around. Had this not been the case, Dante
would have been able to control what he was
feeling for Sophia. She fit perfectly into his
description of beauty. Her style was modest
but sexy, her make up accentuated, it didn't
overpower, her lips maneuvered seductively in

137

speech and seduction. Sophia's eyes teased; staring hard then quickly darting as if diffident. Her shyness was no intrinsic characteristic however; it was another cultivated machination that appealed to man's primitive attraction to a pure, chaste, untouched woman.

Sophia's allure had Lena briefly questioning her own sexuality.

"So are you guys like swingers or something?" Sophia asked.

"No...No..." Dante and Lena said simultaneously.

"Why'd you ask that?" Lena asked.

"O, I don't know, it has to take a lot to ask a perfect stranger to have a threesome. I figured maybe you guys had some experience."

They all smiled.

"No, we're not swingers. Actually this is the first time we've done something this...*crazy* I guess you can say." Dante said before Lena added,

"Yea, we just wanted to try something different. We so happened to have the same fantasy so..."

"So, you decided let's try it; it should keep our sex life interesting." Sophia finished.

"Exactly." Dante said.

"So why me?" Sophia asked.

Lena spoke first.

"Well, it was an easy choice for me. I'm not into women really, I mean, I think they're beautiful creatures but I've never wanted to sleep with one. But, when I saw you I immediately thought, *"If I was into women, this is the type of women I would be with."*

"Well thanks." Sophia responded, reddened by flattery.

"Absolutely, and since we're going to try this it seems like it was meant to be considering the first woman I spotted seems to be a little interested herself..."

139

Sophia smiled.

"Maybe..." She said playfully.

"So, I'm just curious, whose idea was it? Sophia asked.

"It was all her idea." Dante said smiling.

"Well I'm sure you didn't oppose."

"At first I did. I thought it was some kind of joke or test. But you're right, once I saw she was serious, I was all for it."

"What about now? Do you support her choosing me?"

Sophia was sexy and she knew it. She was very much in control of her sexual output. She wasn't some pretty little naïve girl unaware of the powers of her beauty. No, Sophia was well aware of the power her sexuality and allure had over men. She hated to be judged by mere physical attractiveness alone, but she embraced the advantageous nature of it.

Once again Dante downplayed his excitement.

"Yea, I support her..."

140

Sophia smiled. Her meal was done but Lena and Dante were most certainly entertaining and she didn't want this to be the last time the three of them hung out.

"We should get together again real soon; go to a *real* restaurant, get to know each other a little better and discuss this *thing* in a little more detail."

Lena and Dante agreed and the three of them parted ways, each entertaining his and her own thoughts on how this would play out.

PART THREE:

The Meeting

"I really like this place." Sophia said after fully absorbing the ambiance of the hibachi restaurant Lena and Dante had taken her to.

"I'm just upset I've lived here all my life and had no idea it was here."

Tokyo Diner had become a favorite of Dante and Lena's and they figured it was a nice place to get to know Sophia a little more.

"So I take it you guys come here often." Sophia said as the waitress left to fetch waters for the threesome.

"Yea...Dante brought me here for our first date, so...I guess you can say it's a little special to us. So, you said you do like it?"

"Oh yea, it's classy, laid back…I do like it actually." Sophia said before picking up her menu.

"So I'm guessing you two don't play it safe when it comes to the menu…" Sophia smiled mischievously.

"Well, we have been known to experiment a little…" Lena teased.

The threesome blushed with embarrassment but chuckled at the humor and irony of their inside joke.

"Ha haha" Dante said.

"Actually, I play it pretty safe. I try to stick to what I know. Chicken, rice… you know, the usual. Lena on the other hand…"

"So you're the daredevil huh?" Sophia asked Lena.

"I guess I should've known considering this entire thing was your idea…"

Sophia smiled seductively at Lena.

143

"Yea, I guess you can say that ..." Lena said.

"I've always liked to try new things...I just want to live a life rich with experiences, No inhibitions, live and enjoy all life has to offer..."

The stare between Sophia and Lena became instantly intimate.

"Well, thanks to some advice from TLC, I try not to chase waterfalls... I stick to the rivers and the lakes that I'm used to ..." Dante interjected as a hint of jealousy crept into his mind. He had caught the silent exchange between Sophia and Lena. Sometimes a glance says more than words.

"Well, you don't play it too safe..." Sophia said sarcastically.

"I guess you're right." Dante said trying to escape, Sophia's magnetic stare.

After a brief moment of silence it was silently agreed upon that the three of them were ready for the formalities to end and for the act to begin. The meals were finished in

144

relative silence and rather briskly. The coupled exited together and made plans to meet that weekend at a hotel they all agreed upon. It was official; Lena and Dante were really going to go through with this.

PART FOUR:

The Act

Lena was nervous…very nervous, and she had no problem admitting this to Dante as they double-checked their belongings.

"That's completely natural. This is a new thing with a perfect stranger. Say what you want about men but I'm a little nervous my damn self."

"Do you love me?" Lena asked.

"Yes I love you Lena, too much."

"I hope so."

Dante and Lena had reserved the room by phone in Sophia's name so when Sophia showed up to the Crown Plaza Hotel all she had to do was grab her key and make herself comfortable in their suite.

146

Sophia removed her coat and walked towards the bathroom. The shower was nice and it made her smile as she wondered if she and her new friends would make use of it. She smiled at her reflection in the mirror but once again it was one of those smiles that was completely void of humor and merely masked internal pain and confusion. She shook her head in slight disappointment as she thought about how she he had ended up in a hotel room waiting for a strange couple to arrive so she could fulfill their fantasy. This had never been the plan as a child.

Like so many other young women, Sophia's youthful mind had entertained dreams and ambitions of fame and stardom. She wanted to sing, she wanted to model, she wanted to own a fashion line; she wanted to do it all. Then, at eight the molestation began and promiscuity ensued. Then there was the awful

147

rape. O that rape had devastated her and obliterated her love and trust for all men for quite a while. Into the arms of women Sophia had run and into the strip club they had run her. Years of medicating pain and anxiety with drugs followed before she was blessed with a child. The child's existence would inflict a much needed guilt into her that would give her the embarrassment needed to walk away from the underworld and venture into normalcy. Sophia's daughter passed away but not before changing her life. Somehow, her brief appearance and disappearance was seen as ethereal by Sophia and she found it easier than imagined to accept her angel's departure.

Change was wanted but for Sophia, love was needed for this change to take place. She had been treated rather disrespectfully by men over the years and now she was ready to show just how ready to be a wife she was. Her search often bordered on desperation as she tried her hardest to find the love that through it all she had never given up on.

Sophia's past often interfered with her future however and at the moment, like so many other moments in her life, Sophia was alone. Her loneliness had led her into this crazy act.

"Hey...YOLO!" She said smiling. She had brought a bottle of Patroń, and decided to take a shot...well...two, to settle her nerves and get her in the mood.

"Just have fun..." Sophia said to herself before setting her *Pandora* station to *Melanie Fiona* on her phone and kicking back on the sofa.

"I don't know Dante, don't you feel a little...I don't know...sluttish?" Lena said as they stopped at the entrance of the Crown Plaza.

"Sluttish?" Dante said, teasing Lena.

"You know what I mean."

"No, I know and we both know we're not like this, we don't run around doing this every day. You got an idea...a *great* idea..."

"Shut up." Lena said elbowing Dante in the ribs. He laughed.

"It's ok baby, we're the only ones that know anyway."

"I guess you're right..."

Lena and Dante opened the door to the suite and both of them stopped in their tracks. Sophia was on the bed fully nude. She was gently massaging herself.

"I wanted to make it easy for you guys to get comfortable. Don't think just do. Undress and join me."

It was strange at first but even in the beginning there were flashes of pleasure that made Lena know she would enjoy this just as much as Dante if not more. Dante was already enjoying himself. His lips were on Sophia's and his hands were on Lena's backside. Sophia stroked Dante's manhood and Lena timidly rubbed Sophia's breast. A condom appeared. Arousal heightened, the act began.

Dante started with his fiancé, making love to her in the normal missionary fashion. Had it not been for Sophia's hands all over him and Lena, Dante may have been satisfied with making love to his woman again. Sophia however was not willing to play spectator for very long. She became aggressive; dominant. Rolling Dante over, she straddled him and began to make love to him wildly. The wildness was tamed however when she glanced into Dante's eyes and saw what she thought was much more than lust. His touch became gentle and his sex became love-making. Sophia felt wonderful and now she could see just how wonderful she felt to him. Lena saw this and cut back in.

Dante made love to Lena from behind but never took his eyes off of Sophia who made love to herself with her fingers without ever looking away from Dante. Lena was pleasured but obviously distracted; distracted by the chemistry she had picked up on between Dante and Sophia.

Gently, Dante pushed Lena to the side and crawled towards Sophia. She slid beneath him and Dante began to make love to Sophia like a man in love.

No longer was her mind blinded by the bright lights of fantasy. No, now what hovered low was a dark cloud of reality. The clouds of delusion were fading and the fog of illusion was lifted. The reality that lay before Lena was now frightening. This woman, who was really no more than a stranger, was having an orgasm. Sophia's body and soul were momentarily one with her fiancé's. Jealous rage consumed her and her arousal quickly subsided. She was ready for this to be over.

Lena was now questioning why she had suggested this. She was upset but how mad could she be? She brought it up. Lena's eyes fought back tears as she watched Dante make love to Sophia just as passionately as he had done with her so many times.

Dante and Sophia had gotten so lost in each other that neither noticed that Lena was no longer participating. Slowly Lena crawled out of the bed. After untangling her panties from Sophia's she slid them on and reached under the bed for her bra. As she did Sophia's moaning grew louder and she began to climax again. Dante sat back with an egoistic smile on his face as he too was in bliss after bringing Sophia to another orgasm. It was at this point that he glanced to his side and caught the liquid stare of Lena who was finally dressed.

Lena shook her head and walked towards the door.

"Wait...where you goin?"

Lena smiled one of the smiles that merely disguise a frown.

"Nice meeting you." She said to Sophia.

"Love you." She mouthed to Dante before walking out.

"Lena!" Dante called out but Sophia quickly placed her finger on Dante's lips.

"Let her go...we still have the moment..."

Sophia moved her finger and bit down on Dante's bottom lip nearly drawing blood. Slowly she regained her rhythm and began her dance again. Again, Lena had faded from Dante's memory.

Lena's insecurity had only made Sophia more confident. Before Lena's abrupt departure Sophia hadn't felt as if she could have Dante alone but now she did. Sophia's forlorn heart wanted to feel special. She

154

wanted to feel the love Lena felt and she would try her hardest to make Dante fall in love. Her moaning became a sonnet, her riding became a dance; her stream became a river and her sighs became cries. She scratched red streams of passion down his back and arms destined to leave her mark. Satisfied that she had done so physically and mentally, she rode the waves of orgasm then collapsed onto Dante's chest. Dante knew he should leave…right then…he should leave and go after his fiancé…but he didn't.

Sophia nestled closely to Dante's heaving chest, wrapping her arms comfortably around his warm torso. His ripped abdomen was still flexing thanks to his sexual workout and Sophia felt that even in exhaustion he looked gorgeous. If Adonis was the pinnacle of male beauty than Dante was the almond version and now in this moment of beautiful silence, he was all hers. She would not worry herself with how long this moment would last; she would only enjoy the fact that she was living in it.

The silence was slightly uncomfortable for Dante however. What was he supposed to do or say now to his new paramour? Sophia was still a stranger. They hadn't had much of a conversation before this took place. Then there was the dread of what Lena must have been thinking; what she must have been feeling.

The blissful clouds of fantasy were again dissipating, only to be replaced by an overcast of gray reality clouds. This may be the last time Dante and Sophia would see each other and experience the euphoric ecstasy of sexual freedom unencumbered by societal norms. It was now time to return to the normalcy of monogamy, a normalcy that would now inevitably seem mundane in contrast to the titillating debauchery they had just experienced.

The quest for opus magnum

For Sophia, the feelings were more possessive, more attached. It's easier to be a guest than a host; to enter than to permit entrance. To accept an invitation to a sacred temple pales in comparison to inviting a stranger into one. No matter how much times change it seems women still cling to a lover more than a man and Sophia, though she thought she would be stronger, was falling victim to this inability to write sex off as just sex. In her eyes, the act was still sacred and the person she enjoyed it with just as much so. There was no way she would allow this to be the last time she made love to Dante. In a time of hyper masculinity and selfishness, men seemed to be so out of tune with their inner artist, with their poetic nature and sensual side. This, in Sophia's eyes, had men out of tune with the makeup of a woman and how to truly be great lovers. An orgasm seemed to be hard

157

to come by nowadays and now that Dante had guided her to not one but three, she was enamored.

After the cinematic break from her last lover, Sophia's sex life had been reduced to masturbation and synthetic stimulation. She had tried watching pornography but in her eyes, it was too animalistic. There was no passion just what resembled wild animals copulating and men who could care less about what the woman was feeling. At times it appeared degrading and she realized it usually turned her off more than on. Toys were fine until those brief moments of realization kicked in and she would glimpse at her reflection in the mirror. She felt she looked so desperate, weird even, with these battery charged rubber and plastic objects that were supposed to serve as replacements for the real thing. Sometimes a bit of shame would flush through her. Her favorite lover now was merely her manicured fingers and vivid imagination.

The quest for opus magnum

Now that Sophia had experienced the intense passion of a man again, she was addicted. Something about the climactic pleasure was driving Sophia to the cliffs of insanity. The passion was building, she was climbing, and the climax had left her staring over the edge into a dark canyon of irrationality. It was becoming impossible for the screams of rationale to talk her out of jumping. Already at the point of no return, her mind and emotions took a plunge into that abyss of crazed infatuation. Sophia was now falling into that bottomless pit of darkness known as love where few hearts make it out of.

PART FIVE:

The Aftermath

Dante walked slowly to the door. He felt like a sheep being led to a slaughter. He knew an explosive argument was inevitable.

"After seeing how I left, seeing how I felt, you still decided to stay the night with her?"

Dante was shaking his head in disappointment. How did he let Sophia seduce him into staying with her all night? No matter how good she was, how beautiful she was, or how new the feeling was, his loyalty was to Lena and he should have stopped as soon as Lena left. Instead, he allowed his hormones to navigate his course.

"Lena, I'm sorry baby, I fell asleep."

"I left at 10:00 Dante... 1O o' clock!" It's now 10:00am; you stayed with her another 12 hours! Was it that good?"

"C'mon Lena Don't do that to me..."

"Don't do what to you, tell you the truth."

"It was your idea in the first place." Dante reasoned in his own defense.

"Lena was briefly silenced, it was her idea, and what a stupid one. What made her believe she could share the man she loved and cherished? As far as she knew Dante had never cheated and now she had given him permission to sleep with another woman. She was so angry with herself but this didn't excuse Dante staying out all night with this stranger.

"Listen, listen, Lena... I made a mistake and I'm sorry"... This whole thing was a mistake. He added hoping to clandestinely shift some of the blame. He always had to remind Lena that this was all her idea.

161

"Let's just put it behind us now, please. We still have a wedding to plan, children to make, and a home to build. I got caught up in the moment but Lena, you have my heart. I'm not leaving you and I'm willing to fight hard as hell for you not to leave me!

"Look" Dante said grabbing Lena's shoulder to settle her nervous shaking...

"We tried something. It didn't go right. I let it go too far. I should've stopped when you stopped. I didn't and I'm sorry for that. Can we just move on? I'm telling you I want you! Believe that, know that, and trust that! Cause I mean it!"

Dante forced Lena to stare directly into his eyes.

"Ok?"

After some hesitation, Lena nodded yes. The surrender was actually a relief for Lena who exhaled a heavy load of resentment. What could she do, it was what it was. She was at blame for introducing the idea in the first place.

162

After a few weeks, things returned to normal and though they hadn't forgotten what had happened, they had found a way to put it behind them. One of the things they had done to do so was fishing. They would get into fishing and get away together every Sunday. Lena could read and Dante could busy himself with the oft-tedious task of catching fish.

It was one of their routine outings when Sophia showed up at their home.

"Hey babe, let's go! The earlier the better."

"I'm coming, I'm coming." Lena shouted from their bedroom as she touched up her face in the vanity mirror.

Dante Walked outside to load the car. As he tried to remain focused on fish, and bait, and location, and technique a woman who had been jogging nearby stopped and called his name.

"Dante?" The woman asked. She wanted to be sure she wasn't mistaking the man for someone else.

Dante recognized the woman immediately and his heart dropped. Instinctively his head spun towards the house to make sure Lena wasn't looking out of any windows.

"Sophia what are you doing here?"

"I was just taking a jog that's all."

"Stop with the bullshit you don't even live in this neighborhood."

"Dante why are you ignoring me like this?"

"Sophia, because I can't..."

"Yes you can. And you want to. Sophia glanced over in time to see Lena walking out of the house. She quickly handed Dante a card.

"Call me!" She said before putting on her earphones and jogging away.

"What are you looking at?" Lena said as she made her way to the car.

164

"And who was that?"

"Hah, umm I don't know, some woman. I wasn't looking."

"Ahh, hah, some woman..." Lena said skeptically.

"And you were looking; you almost broke your neck."

That close call was not enough to keep Dante from calling Sophia. Just seeing her again had brought back so many memories. He couldn't fight the urge this time. And this time, he gave into temptation and began having an affair with Sophia.

PART SIX:

The Affair

Sophia and Dante began seeing each other as much as often. For Dante, this was strenuous because the more time he spent with Sophia the more time she demanded and it was something he no longer had much of to spare. Being engaged to Lena and still trying to move forward with their plans of unification while at the same time entertaining Sophia's dreams to do the same thing were slowly exhausting him.

No matter how exhausting he couldn't find his way out of the maze he was now in. Sophia was very deep and her love was deeper. It was an ocean that Dante submerged himself in every chance he could. Sophia was a mystery that piqued his curiosity and the regret he often felt was simply not enough to stop him from entertaining this curiousness.

Besides the mystery was the reality. Sophia's soul had been tortured thus far in life. Abused by men and misused by life, her heart was now a shadow of its once radiant self. She had become very numb. Dante soon found himself wanting to help Sophia; wanting to fix her.

In a fight, Sophia had told Dante,

"You don't really know me."

"I beg to differ." He said, not at all fazed by her warning.

"Why is that?" Sophia had asked, slightly confused by Dante's response.

"To say I don't know you is to say I don't know myself. We're one in the same."

"How do you figure?" Sophia asked.

"How do you figure we're not?" Dante shot right back.

167

Not in the mood to play his game, Sophia said, *"I have a past."* very flatly.

Just as calm and even-toned, Dante replied.

"And so do I. Every rose has its thorns, and he who wants a rose must respect the thorns. One of the most admired flowers can also be one of the most painful...like love...Am I perfect? No, I'm cheating on my fiancé right now..."

The reality of his words stung but Sophia didn't interrupt.

"I'm human too is what I'm saying. If I was in complete control I wouldn't have let this get this far; not because I don't like it but because it's wrong."

And even after admitting it was wrong, Dante made love to Sophia again.

When the two were alone, Sophia felt complete. Dante was now her world and she hated that his love had come at another woman's cost but she couldn't let it go. And even if they were discovered and she was labeled a home wrecker, well, Sophia was fine with that, she had been called worse. And that was a very small price to pay for a lifetime of happiness with such an incredible man.

There were plenty of times where Dante had tried to walk away but often realized he had already gone too far. Sophia was at the point now where any separation would be unbearable. He was now something she would fight for and as crazy as it may have sounded, she now felt Dante was partly hers.

If there was an area in which Lena lacked, she would fill that void. So, Sophia listened closely to Dante's every complaint. If Lena did something wrong, she would do it right. If Lena hadn't exposed him to something yet, she would. He loved to read so she became a writer. Her natural gift for writing was

169

a serendipitous discovery that had begun as nothing more than a ploy to please Dante. It was this power in Dante that Sophia was addicted to; his ability to pull the best out of her.

This tug-a-war love affair would go on for weeks. Dante would always make Sophia believe he would be hers but would always end up letting her down. She knew that it wasn't that he didn't love her; it was that he still owed Lena and felt obligated to her. Selfishly, Sophia no longer cared at what expense Dante's love came and she began to intentionally leave clues, praying Lena would discover the illicit affair and she could finally have Dante to herself.

Dante's mind became dizzy in those few weeks of infidelity. He was under Sophia's spell. He knew it but couldn't fight it. She was slowly making him lose sight of the love he had found in Lena and Lena noticed this more than anyone.

The quest for opus magnum

Dante and Lena had been together for so long that any slight nuance in his behavior was easy to notice. Dante had become absent and a whole lot less affectionate. Any affection he did show felt forced and/or premeditated. Something had come between her and her man but Lena was willing to fight to save their relationship.

Sophia had the same thought in mind and before he knew it, Dante was constantly fighting Lena's allegations, and Sophia's ploys to destroy what was left of his relationship. Sophia was trying everything now from perfuming his clothes to showing up unexpectedly at his job.

"Sophia you can't just be showing up at my job like this." Dante said as he put the flowers down in the backseat of Sophia's Camry.

"And why would you have the flowers delivered? You could've just given them to me this weekend."

"Well I didn't feel like waiting to the weekend and I thought you may appreciate it. Sorry, I won't do anything nice anymore. I'll continue to hide and be available to you only when you want to see me."

"C'mon Sophia, don't do that."

"Do what Dante? It's the truth. You want to see me when you want to see me, what about when I get the urge to see you? Like today, I thought about you, so I got you some flowers to show you and I actually did hand deliver them I just asked your partner to give them to you because I knew you wouldn't want me coming in there. So actually, I was thinking, and I was mindful of your situation but why don't you ever consider or care for how I may feel. Dante, do you have any idea how I feel at night when you're not with me? To know that you're holding her, caressing her, telling her you love her; do you have any idea how it feels to love someone but have to *hope* they answer your calls, well your *texts* because you're not *allowed* to call? You don't! You text, I text right back and if you call I come running. And now, I can't even do things to show my affection for you? Do you know you told me you love me Dante?"

"Yes Sophia, of course I know what I told you."

"Do you know what that means? And not just what it means but what it means to a person who has been so deprived of it. Do you know you can hurt people Dante? I've been hurt, by men who said they loved me but they had an ulterior motive. You said you were different, but are you...really?"

"Of course I am Sophia, you know I am..."

173

"No I thought you were, but what I'm starting to realize is you have the same ulterior motive. Sex is the ultimate agenda; you're just clever enough to mask your intentions."

"No I'm not…"

"Yes you are Dante. You use me as an emotional and sexual escape from Lena. The sad part is I can see how this ends. Soon you'll get tired of my sex, as all men do with women, but unlike Lena, there will be nothing to keep you connected to me. No children, no engagement. You know I'll be hurt, but you'll reason that I'll get over it in time and slowly you'll push me out of your mind. I know how this story plays out; I've seen the movie a thousand times."

Guilt was killing Dante. He really did love Sophia, and he now realized he had let this go on to the point that there was no way this would end on a good note. Someone was going to get hurt, very badly.

"Listen, Sophia, I don't just tell you I love you for sex, or, just for the sake of saying it..."

"Well why do you say it?"

"Because, I mean it."

"Prove it." Sophia said stubbornly. She was slowly growing tired of Dante's inability to make up his mind. Making up one's mind is not the hard part however, making up one's heart was a lot more difficult. The mind submissively follows the convictions of the heart.

"How?"

"Follow your heart."

"I did, and it got me in this mess."

"Mess, wow, just last night it was beauty, now it's a mess?"

"That's not what I mean..."

"That's what you said."

"Stop! Sophia, I'm not perfect and obviously I'm not heartless. If I was heartless I would have done the right thing and stopped this affair, admitted it to my fiancé, and begin work on making things right if she was willing to. I don't want to hurt you or her."

"Well soon Dante, you're not going to have a choice, you're gonna have to make a decision and one of us is gonna have to deal with the pain of loss…"

"Or we can all end up dealing with loss…"

Sophia went silent. She could only push so much. In the end, she didn't want to lose Dante or do anything to make him contemplate leaving her. No matter how much she appeared to be making an ultimatum, she knew it was weightless. It was her attempt to appear in control of a situation she realized she wasn't. She wouldn't have ever left Dante, he would have to leave her, and even that would be hard.

"Look Sophia, I'm trying to figure this out and if you want me to leave you alone to do it I will…"

176

The quest for opus magnum

That was exactly what Sophia *didn't* want to hear. Knowing her bluff had been called and she had been defeated, Sophia's shoulders dropped along with her head. Where was her dignity going? She asked herself as she mumbled,

"No, that's not what I want..."

"It's enough that you show up at my house, at... but now you're compromising my livelihood. This is how I survive, how I feed myself and my family. You're taking this too far. Sophia, this has to end; for the sake of everyone involved."

"How am I taking this too far? Dante maybe you should've thought about that before you agreed to this. I'm not just some worthless object you can throw away whenever you're done. What, now that I satisfied your lust for something you were missing at home, you're

177

ready to get rid of me? It doesn't work like that Dante."

"That's exactly how it works Sophia. We agreed to a fling, not a relationship."

"You labeled it a fling, I just agreed to wanting to see you again."

"Whatever the case, this situation was supposed to be a no-strings affair..."

"Why are you being so mean to me right now..."

A pang of guilt shot through Dante's heart as tears began to well up in Sophia's eyes.

"I'm sorry..."

"Dante, you make love to me like I'm your wife, is it my fault you get caught up in the passion? I mean, I can't help that my feelings for you have grown."

"Sophia you're right... I know... and I'm sorry. That's not what I wanted to happen."

"Well that's what happened and I know I can't have you exclusively but you can't just ditch me like this Dante, You just can't do that... Like, what did I do?"

"Sophia, it's not what you did...I mean showing up at my place was definitely not cool but that's not it, it's not something you did, it's the fact that I'm engaged."

"I understand that and I'm fine with it."

"You're fine with knowing I have a fiancé, soon a wife, and the fact that there may be no chance of a future with us?"

"Yes."

"C'mon Sophia..."

"No, I'm serious, I really love you Dante and I'd rather have some of you then none of you, since I can't have all of you."

Dante paused. Sophia's last statement made him realize just how infatuated Sophia had become. Dante labeled it infatuation because the love Sophia was proclaiming was not a love that was exclusive for him. This was

179

a void in her soul that she was trying to fill and he just so happened to fit. That was all he could reason as he tried to wrap his mind around Sophia's desperation.

"Sophia C'mon, you have to have more pride in yourself than that, you know, some dignity. You're telling me your fine with just being my thing on the side..."

"No, that's what you're saying. I'm saying I'll wait, six months, a year, whatever it takes to make you realize that you should be with me. I'm not fine with being second, but I'm fine with waiting my turn to be first."

Dante was going to respond, but noticed his lunch break was over.

"We'll finish this later."

"I hope so." Sophia said.

Dante got up to leave and Sophia was going to let him, but she couldn't. She never could.

"Are you really that mad at me? No kiss?"

180

Dante shook his head and smiled at the irony. Sophia felt Dante was obligated to treat her exactly as he would Lena. She wasn't wrong for this; he had told her he loved her.

"Of course." Dante said before leaning over to extend a kiss.

"So I'll see you later than?" Sophia asked.

"Yes."

PART SEVEN:

The Discovery

Lena double-checked her appearance in the driver side window of her car. It had been a while since she had shown up to Dante's job unexpected but she knew it was one of the sacrifices she would have to make to get her man's full attention again. They hadn't even as much as spoken about the wedding after their episode with Sophia and Lena was starting to worry Dante may have been getting cold feet.

Lena reached into the backseat and grabbed the single rose and card she bought him. In the passenger seat was a platter of seafood for his lunch. Gathering everything she had brought Dante, Lena checked her watch…

"Dang!" She mumbled. Her tucked lips were clenching on the card she now held with her mouth. She was late and wouldn't be able to spend lunch with Dante like she had planned. Still, she hustled her way into the building in case Dante was still on his lunch.

Once inside one of Dante's co-workers, knowing who Lena was, greeted her than offered to get him for her. He had already returned to work. As he was turning on his heels the sight of the rose finally processed and Julius smiled and said,

"Oh, forgot one huh? Dante must be a real good dude, you came all the way back to bring him one rose…how sweet."

Lena looked confused and Julius realized immediately that he had made a mistake. Nervousness now shook his heart and beads of sweat began to accumulate on his brow. How would he get out of this? Not only was Lena now flaming with rage, Dante would be to once he found out who was responsible for his fiancé discovering his affair.

"What are you talking about?" Was all Lena could come up with, although she was very aware of what the man was saying. Someone had already brought Dante flowers and the thought of who it may have been was destroying Lena inside.

"Nuh…nothing…"

"No, don't stutter and don't get amnesia all of a sudden, you were just so articulate and charming. Maybe the fact that you're about to lie to me is causing some difficulty inside…"

"Look…I don't know, who, what…look I don't know anything, all I know is Dante came from break with some flowers, that's it. I just assumed they were from you."

"And now you realize they weren't and that you messed up."

184

Julius was silent. He knew it was best to quit while he was ahead and not say anything else that may get him into deeper waters.

"What did she look like?"

Julius just ignored her and led the way to where Dante was working. He asked Lena to hold on as he summoned Dante.

Dante smiled when Julius called his name but when he saw the look on Julius's pale face, he knew something was wrong.

"Wassup bro, you look like you saw a ghost."

"Not a ghost...the devil himself." Julius thought as he hung his head in shame.

"I messed up man. I had no idea someone else brought you flowers...your fiancé came in and I mentioned them..."

"And now I want to know who the hell is bringing my man flowers to his job?" Lena interjected furiously.

185

Dante's eyes shot to Lena's they were bloodshot; then to Julius's, they were guilt-ridden; then to the flowers…they spoke without speaking.

"Excuse us." Dante said to Julius.

"My bad man…"

"Just go, it's cool." Dante said. No matter how upset he wanted to be with Julius he knew he couldn't. His infidelity had gotten him into this; Julius's big mouth was just the conduit through which Karma manifested itself.

"Lena…"

"WHO?"

"Listen…"

"WHO?"

Everything inside of Dante was saying lie; make up a story; it could've been anyone; compliments of the company; anything… He couldn't however manufacture a satisfactorily lie in the brief millisecond in which Lena would be expecting a reply. So, he spewed the truth…some of it.

The quest for opus magnum

"Listen Lena, Sophia found me somehow. She found out where I worked and she wanted to drop some flowers off. Probably not smart but she actually mentioned you and said she was just thinking about us and wanted to express it. I mean, it is flowers, and I am a man, so maybe they were meant more for..."

"Don't play with me Dante, are you seeing this woman?"

"No."

"Let me see your phone."

"My phone?"

"Yes, *your phone*, let me see it."

Dante complied. He had long deleted any messages that had been exchanged between him and Sophia.

After a brief search that produced zero evidence, Lena gave Dante his phone back.

"Why is she bringing you flowers Dante? Why is she even still around?"

187

Dante answered these questions and what seemed to be a hundred more by the night's end.

By the next morning the suspicion had grown into conviction. There was no way that woman just showed up without some prior communication with Dante. If it was one thing Lena knew, men will often try to play the *Stalker Card* when caught cheating; that being, labeling the mistress a stalker to relieve themselves of any guilt. True, some women did get *stalkerish*, but only after their feelings have been somehow toyed with.

Lena was right, as she followed Dante that next week she would discover that not only was he still seeing Sophia, but he was now the pursuer. Once that week he had gone shopping at Macy's for her. Twice he had gotten her flowers. He had taken her to dinner, and even managed to attend a carnival in a town twenty minutes from where they lived.

188

Lena found two things odd; one was how fast Dante would get to Sophia, it wasn't as if they spent much time apart, the other was how oblivious he was to her following him. His thoughts in that period were too consumed with Sophia and his illicit affair with her.

What was killing her inside was how genuinely happy appeared to be with Sophia. This is what hurt the most. It made her question herself, even though she knew she had no reason to. And now watching her man spend time, blissfully, with another woman was killing her. And even after being confronted with pictures and evidence, Dante went back to Sophia the very next week. Lena could see it in Dante's eyes, he was in love. Of course she knew the look because she had melted in its flattery early in their relationship as well. It was a look he held only for her until they met Sophia. No, Lena would not lose her man

189

without a fight. She had already lost his love; she could feel and see that. But now, with Sophia in the way they would never be able to regain that love. This thought was driving Lena mad. Eventually, it would drive her to murder.

PART EIGHT:

The End

As Lena made her way towards the door, drenched in rain, and soaked in pain, a terror began to rise in her chest as she realized she was afraid of the monster this situation had created. She had never been a violent soul; competitive but not combative. Violence in movies bothered her; let alone real life violence. Yet here she was, gun in hand, vendetta in mind, and prepared to take the life of the woman that had stolen her love away.

Lena knew the two were here alone in this Bungalow as she had followed Dante every day for the past week. She had taken a leave of absence from work and had unfortunately, confirmed what she knew to be

191

true. Dante had continued seeing Sophia. They were having an affair.

Lena raised her hand to knock on the door but apprehension stopped her from knocking. A myriad of emotions dizzied Lena's confused mind. She feared embarrassment, humiliation, degradation; she feared many things but not enough to not go through with this. She had been destroyed by pain and it was time for someone else to experience it.

A hesitant knock was followed by three booming ones that startled the illicit lovers inside. Panic overtook Sophia and Dante immediately. No one was supposed to know they were here so who could be knocking of this hour? They both began suffering from the same dreadful thought; it was Lena at the door. She was scorned and broken hearted and she probably had hate in her heart and revenge in her eyes.

Sophia sat up in bed and pulled the sheets closely to her body.

"Put your robe on." Dante whispered as he crept through the house to the window in order to get a good look at their visitor. Because of the rain, darkness, and angle of the window, Dante was unable to see who it actually was. He could see that the person was small in stature; most likely a woman, and most likely Lena. His heart fluttered and Sophia sensed the paranoia.

"Is it her?" Sophia asked.

"I think so."

"What are you gonna do?"

"You have to hide."

"Hide" Sophia questioned upset.

"I'm not some teenage girl sneaking in to your mom's house. I'm not hiding…"

"Sophia, not now!"

"No, Dante, I'm tired of hiding, it's time for you to be a man and tell her how you feel about me."

193

"Not now; not like this. It would hurt her too much."

Again there was a loud thud at the door followed by a shock to Dante's heart.

"What about me Dante. Why are you always pushing my feelings aside to protect hers? Why do you care more about how she feels then I do? I love you too Dante... Why do you do this to me? You get me all excited, like you love me and really wanna be with me but..."

Dante fell silent. He had no rebuttal. He had allowed Sophia to fall in love and now he was paying for it double-fold. His fiancé was at the door in pain and Sophia was now in tears as well.

Again there was a knock but this time it was followed by a voice ordering Dante to open the door. If there was any doubt left it was gone now; that was most definitely Lena at the door.

Dante took a deep breath and proceeded to the door. He looked back at Sophia once more before turning the knob. She simply shook her head no and said,

"I'm not hiding."

Dante was no longer going to fight it. Sophia was right. He had to face Lena. He had to tell her the truth. He had to tell her what he felt for Sophia but once he opened the door. He couldn't.

Lena's mascara had trailed below her cheek, adding emphasis to her streams of tears. She was hurt, beyond repair, and the pain and shame it caused Dante was unbearable. There was no way he could hurt her. They had shared so much of life together. They had so many memories, and now he was reminded of this.

"Where is she?" Lena asked.

"Lena, Listen…" As Dante tried to place his hands on Lena's shoulder to calm her, Sophia called out…

"Baby who is it? Come back to bed." It was intentional; she was tired of hiding and playing this game. If Dante wasn't going to tell Lena he loved her, she would! Dante dropped his head and shook it as he anticipated what was next. He would only have a second to ponder Lena's next move. She stepped back and kicked as hard as she could at the door. Her eyes were like those of a raging bull's and for the first time ever. Dante was genuinely afraid of Lena.

In that split second of heightened fear, Dante missed the shiny metallic object in Lena's hand but it was clearly visible now. Sophia was screaming, squirming around in the bed, with her hands in front of her, she plead with Lena not to kill her; Dante began to do the same.

196

"Lena...Lena...take it easy...Please... think about what you're doing..."

Lena was dead silent. She hadn't responded at all to what Dante was saying, nor to Sophia's pleads; only the voice of vengeance telling her she would never be satisfied until she avenged her honor.

"Lena...you can't just kill somebody...it won't end here Lena, think...it ends in a courtroom Lena, with you going to prison forever. Nobody's worth that...not even me."

His words fell on deaf ears. Dante could see that Lena had blocked out the world and all she could see was Sophia...Dying.

"Lena No!" Dante said as he watched, Lena's fingers gripping tighter around the trigger.

Dante quickly stepped in front of the gun.

"Why are you protecting her Dante? Why are you protecting *HER*!?"

"Lena, I'm protecting you! You don't have to do this. I see how hurt you are and that's enough. You don't have to go any further."

Dante looked back at Sophia.

"It's over Sophia. Do you see what this is causing us all? I don't care what happened or how it happened it has to stop." Sophia dropped her head knowingly. No matter what she felt, Dante was right. Sophia was a woman and she now felt this woman's pain.

"Lena, give me the gun."

"Ok." Lena said. Her tensed muscles relaxed and she surrendered the weapon to Dante.

"It's gonna be..."

Before Dante could say *"ok"* There was a loud blast. Dante stared deep into Lena's eyes and whispered..."

"Sorry..."

198

The quest for opus magnum

A gush of blood spewed from his mouth and he swooned to the floor. Sophia screamed. She had covered her mouth but the cries were far from muffled. Lena drifted back in freight and disbelief. Her eyes were wide with shock. Her mouth too was wide open but not a sound escaped her lips. Terrified, her trembling fingers finally released the gun and it fell to the floor.

Sophia flew off the bed and pressed as hard as she could at the wound. It was spilling blood too quickly for her hands to cover. She began speaking to Dante calmly and Lena watched in silence from the shadows. She was paralyzed by shock.

Holding his limp body in her arms, Sophia felt guilt. Yet staring over at the woman that had shot him, she felt rage. Dante had brought Sophia back to life; he had stitched her torn heart. He made her dream again and gave

199

her hope. He gave her strength, taught her and most importantly, he had loved her. She would never forgive herself knowing she could have prevented this horrible accident.

The guilt doubled as Sophia stared into the dimming eyes of the man she felt was her only true lover. The sirens sounded too far away to save him. She wanted to leave but hope made her stay. Hope that Dante wouldn't die here like this. He didn't deserve it. Bullets, blood, and the stench of death; it wasn't supposed to be like this. She wasn't even supposed to love him.

Dante choked on a clot of blood and continued to grimace in pain. He tried to speak but couldn't. Instead, that was how he died, struggling to find the right words to explain how he had loved them both no matter how wrong or right, and how he had only wanted to make them both feel special.

200

Cocoons

O caterpillar, O caterpillar. Why do you stare at the butterfly in wonder and amazement...do you not realize it is in your nature to become the very same thing? No need to worship the majesty of that which you too can become. You merely have to overcome your fear of cocoons...

Saleem Little

My American Dream

With my bird's eye view from the talons of an
eagle
I spy the recipe for Manifest Destiny
The boats at the docks, the chains, bolted
locks
A trader at an auction bidding on the strongest
Ox
But the Ox is not a cattle it's a man viewed as
chattel
Lost eyes, lost soul and an auctioneer's gavel
Sold! To Mr. William Lynch from the shores of
Virginia...
The forlorn can't communicate physically or
mentally

The quest for opus magnum

Ritually or literally or linguistically
Chunks of sun tanned flesh cling to strips of
animal hide
Strange fruits dangle high,
Strangled cries from mangled eyes
Terrorist! Terrorist! Takes one to know one
Dictator! Dictator! Every soil grows one
Tyrant! Tyrant! Every nation knows one
Some had no choice; some with free votes
chose one...
We fly to the land of Pharaohs
To visit the eagle's uncle Horus
The scenes identical, the workers followers of
Moses,
Praying for an exodus, praying for an exorcist
Once freed they worship worthless gold calves
and necklaces

Saleem Little

Then we landed on a house with a white picket
fence
Two children and a dog that turn to dust then
dispense
The stares of greedy bankers turn my dream
into a nightmare
Rats racing, rabbits chasing carrots
Heightened fright and fear
A hypnotizing box tells me status means
everything
Then rolls quickly flashing images
Of cars and diamond rings
Bling! Bling! there's a twinkle and I awake
How'dthe dream I've always loved
Become a nightmare that I hate...

The quest for opus magnum

Mercados

Melted cheese and tomato sauce
40 ounces and faded memories
Hopelessness permeates the ambiance
It chokes my optimistic lungs
Futile chatter of how dreams were shattered
By imperialistic reality and lottery scratching
I pause to suck cool air through clenched teeth
Dried peppers sting like the pungent scent of
perspiration
Neon lights for Coors Light
An invite to forget life
Or maybe to remember...
Used to be a swingin' spot

Saleem Little

Bustling with youth hungry for pepperonis and
mushrooms
The merchants were younger then
The patrons too
The jukebox blared some eighties tune
I was the breakdance kid on a pizza box
dancefloor
Spinning on my head and, guess what I
danced for
A slice so hot that it burned the top
Of my mouth
One of my favorite pains
In my favorite pizza shop

Careful

Be careful of the careless who invite you to
their apathy
When you shed a tear of care and your
ventricles tear
They tell you to care less but the fearless fear
less
The careful are full of care while the careless
care less
Some tears break down while some build up
Hard for those full of care and the careless to
build trust
My pain is not a strain it's a motivating force
Like a whip to the hip just motivates the horse

Saleem Little

Saw a man in Syria
Holding his daughter's bomb riddled body
And with no remorse
A man told me that wasn't his problem
My eyes were close to tears
His eyes were summer air
Dry, no sign of care
Mine blinded by despair
I trace life to one source so see humanity as
family
He said this way of thinking
Would just jeopardize my sanity
Told me I should be careful, I'm too full of care
Hard to take advice from one who seems
emotionally impaired...

The quest for opus magnum

0

Climax...
The Pinnacle of arousal
Is my speech alone orgasmic enough to
arouse you
The espousal of the passionate atmosphere
around you
And a mind determined to eternally astound
you
A reciprocation of scintillating stimulation
Emanating from titillating penetration
A verbal discourse
A Mental intercourse
While the waves of a silken sea
Crash into a shore...
Of estrogen

The quest for opus magnum

Oxygen...
Breathe...
Regroup...
Tongues morph into serpents
Dancing to a charmer's flute
Nothing sweeter than the scent of sweat
Produced by passion
Glistening bodies moonlit
On a War torn mattress
Trickles of blood on my back, biceps and chest
Blush hand prints on her posterior
Bite marks on her neck
Blood on her lips, hair on my fingers
Sound mixes with scent in the air and it
lingers...
Her eyes become wide as her levees explode
No more sounds from her lips
They just form an O

Saleem Little

The Great Mistake

From observation to contemplation
Is ovulation God's creation?
Or another mistake blown out of proportion
Explicable in theories with scientific origins
From Zero came one from one explosion
From *bang* to brain matter conscious of motion
The explosion created no chaotic mess
But harmonious sets of complex concepts
Guess theologians merely pray to matter
For matter's the God that entropy scatters
Created itself and is self-sustained
My God that was sure one intelligent *bang*…

The quest for opus magnum

Enemies

I was once asked why I so often pardon my
enemies,
Well for one I have long been an enemy of
myself
Grateful that my higher self, pardoned the
animalistic desires of my lower self
And that my higher power forgave both.
Beyond this I have realized that most enemies
are not enemies at all.
A male victim of my smiting
A woman that I've slighted
Who feels "friend or foe you will acknowledge I
exist."

Saleem Little

Most of my enemies
Are former friends of me
Aroused to envy
Or friends I've treated indifferently
My enemies…
The competitive edge of a man's ego and pride
The vindictive pledge in a woman's jaded mind
Critics who misinterpret my dimensions
And my purpose of intentions
Whose shallow minds only see
The surface of my missions…
Hatred is a blanket that covers admiration
For the ego sees praise as a veil too thin

Life after Death

All things in human society pass on in time due to the insatiable desires of the human ego. Materialism and synthetic forms of communication and entertainment will soon fade as well. All things have their season. Soon the natural life will again prevail…like spring after winter…life after death…

Saleem Little

Legacy

What do you want to leave behind? Is it a great building that men can stare up at in awe, maybe smart, intelligent, successful children, is it a legacy in the field you choose as a career. For me, I just want to leave words that remind and inspire. The transmitting of knowledge is a perpetual and eternal race that will continue whether you grab the baton or not... I want to be in that race; not as a spectator, and most certainly not as the track of falsehood being trampled by the stampede of truths racing to the ultimate finish line...

The quest for opus magnum

All the praises and thanks be to the Most High, Lord of all the worlds and everything that exist therein. My Mother, my children and my siblings, my friends though few, I cherish your patience…And thank you to everyone who had a dream and chased it. In doing so you inspired me to chase mine. To everybody who supports me…Thank you.

Saleem Little

Coming Soon...

The quest for opus magnum

2015...

Saleem Little

PRESENTS

  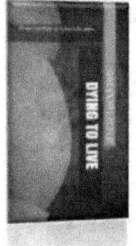

THE TRILOGY

220

The quest for opus magnum

221

www.ingramcontent.com/pod-product-compliance
Lightning Source LLC
Chambersburg PA
CBHW071506170626
46811CB00007B/2745